Fan-Powered Futures
Shaping the Future of Spotify and Times Square through Fan Innovation

By Nick Holmstén

Copyright © 2024 by Nick Holmstén

All rights reserved.

No part of this book may be reproduced, distributed, or transmitted in any form or by any means, including photocopying, recording, or other electronic or mechanical methods, without the prior written permission of the publisher, except in the case of brief quotations embodied in reviews and certain other non-commercial uses permitted by copyright law.

DISCLAIMER: Spotify has not partnered with the author on this book, nor has it approved the content. The book contains the author's own recollections and opinions.

Dedication

To my beloved family,

To my parents, Monica and Oscar, you are not around anymore, but I'm grateful for all the support, love, and values you taught me. I hope I made you proud and that you can follow my journey even after you leave this world.

To my brother Mikael, for being by my side through life's ups and downs.

To my best friend and partner for life, Marie, I love you! Your unwavering support and love have been my rock, guiding me through every challenge and triumph.

And to our two amazing and good-hearted children, Enni and Elton, you are my everything! Your laughter, love, and zest for life fill my days with joy and purpose.

Lastly, to Chloe, our family's beloved dog, who always brings happiness and love to our home through good times and hard times. Your loyal companionship and wagging tail remind us of the simple joys and unconditional love that make our family complete.

This book is dedicated to all of you, my pillars of strength and sources of inspiration.

Table of Contents

Introduction 7

Chapter 1: A Life in Harmony: My Journey from Swedish Roots to Global Tunes 10

Chapter 2: The Playlist Revolution: Tunigo's Acquisition by Spotify 30

Chapter 3: At the Helm of a Revolution: Leading Spotify's Global Music Domination 37

Chapter 4: A Year with Drake and Lady Gaga That Changed Everything 58

Chapter 5: What Came Next: Times Square-Style Entertainment 64

Chapter 6: The Paradigm Shift to Fan Engagement 72

Chapter 7: The Roots of Passion – A Brief History of Fandom 84

Chapter 8: From Disney to TSX: Crafting a Legacy of Fandom 90

Chapter 9: Post Malone: This is the coolest venue in the f**ing universe 96

Chapter 10: The Global Stage Awakens 102

Chapter 11: The Third Time is a Charm for a New Times Square Dynasty 106

Chapter 12: The TSX Entertainment Odyssey: Pioneering the Future of Entertainment 115

Chapter 13: The Art of Turning Enthusiasts into Superfans 118

Chapter 14: Engaging Hearts and Minds with Storytelling and Authenticity 132

Chapter 15: Fans, Followers, and Superstars:
Technology's Transformative Power 150

Chapter 16: When a Fan-Powered Future
Comes to Life 168

Deep Dive—Sweden's Unstoppable Rise in
Music and Tech 177

Acknowledgments 187

About the Author 189

Introduction

In 2018, I was one of the most powerful people in the music industry.

As the Global Head of Music for Spotify, I was the one interacting with the artists and record labels and building new tools that would change the world and disrupt every paradigm the music industry had ever known. (I even flew to Taylor Swift's Hollywood home to convince her of the value of Spotify. That's right—there once was a time when Swifties had to work a lot harder to hear their queen's music.)

Almost overnight, we went from a world where only four companies and a small group of gatekeepers controlled nearly everything to the Spotify mission of "connect as many artists as possible with as many fans as possible," thanks to the power of data, a lot of innovation, and a completely transformed industry.

In the annals of music history, few moments have been as transformative and disruptive as the advent of music streaming services. The familiar landscape underwent a seismic shift. Spearheaded by platforms like Spotify, this revolution was a technological leap and a cultural and economic upheaval that redefined the essence of music consumption, discovery, and distribution.

The early narrative of music consumption painted record stores as sanctuaries reserved for superfans and connoisseurs, places on where the average listener felt out of place. Streaming services like Spotify dismantled these barriers nearly overnight, offering a welcoming space for both the avid record collector and the casual listener who had previously experienced music primarily through curated radio or television channels.

In the nascent days of Spotify, the platform was a haven for music fanatics. These early adopters reveled in the freedom to create playlists and embark on quests for new musical discoveries.

New listeners, new strategies, new opportunities

However, as streaming edged into the mainstream, it ushered in a whole new wave of listeners. This broader audience sought guidance; they were not necessarily inclined to actively search for music or curate personal playlists. This is where the genius of Spotify's strategy soon became evident.

Recognizing the need for a more guided experience, Spotify introduced its own playlists. I remember telling Daniel Ek, the Co-Founder and CEO of Spotify, following the acquisition of my company Tunigo, "Now that Spotify has its own playlists, we will create playlist brands that will eclipse even the biggest radio stations in the United States."

It was a bold prediction at the time, but it soon became a reality. Playlist brands like RapCaviar, Today's Top Hits, and Viva Latino gained monumental influence, surpassing even the most prominent radio stations in the United States in their ability to break new artists.

Spotify was the savior of a dying industry, and I was fortunate to enjoy and engineer the ride of a lifetime. In my seven years at Spotify, we witnessed a massive shift from traditional sales to a streaming-centric model, fundamentally altering how music reaches fans and how artists achieve stardom.

At this same crazy time, I discovered the power of nurturing fan bases and how unbelievably important it is to forge deep and lasting connections. It is not about consumers anymore—fans are a must. It's all about creating a loyal, engaged community that propels a music artist or any other brand to infinite stardom and fandom. This is the present and the future of the music industry.

As we delve deeper into this book, we will explore the transition from music gatekeepers to fans as the true gatekeeper, understanding how streaming services changed not just how we access music but also how it is created, shared, and monetized. You will also see how today's trends are shaping up to create a fan-forward future for us all.

In "Fan-Powered Futures: Shaping the Future of Spotify and Times Square through Fan Innovation," you will enjoy a front-row and behind-the-scenes real-life adventure of the streaming revolution.

And you might get to learn a little more about Drake, Lady Gaga, The Weekend, and Post Malone along the way…

CHAPTER 1

A Life in Harmony: My Journey from Swedish Roots to Global Tunes

In the charming town of Karlstad, Sweden, my story began, woven with threads of music, culinary adventures, and an early entrepreneurial spirit.

I was born into a family where melodies flowed as freely as conversation, inspiring a lifelong passion for music. My father, Oscar, an electrician and owner of a small firm, and my mother, Monica, a compassionate nurse, instilled in my brother Mikael and me a deep, deep love for music.

Our home was a symphony of sounds and tastes, thanks to parents who were not just guardians but also musicians, and a mother whose culinary experiments brought the world to our table.

Music from the start

By the tender age of 7, I had embarked on my first musical voyage with Mikael and some other childhood friends, forming a band that was more than just a childhood whim. This band, nurtured under the managerial wings of our father, who transported our band in his trusty turquoise Volvo 145, became the early playground of our wildest childhood dreams.

Our four-piece ensemble included Tord Henriksson on drums, Peter Lundin on bass, my brother Mikael juggling guitar and keyboard duties, and me as the lead vocalist. We played wherever opportunity beckoned.

Our set-up, though modest, was a source of immense pride: homemade speakers and amplifiers, with most instruments acquired through mail order. Our distinctly Swedish dance music stood worlds apart from what is commonly known as dance music today. It was, in essence, a quirky blend akin to a cheesy version of country music, yet distinctly ours with its Swedish lyrics.

Our audiences were often small, sometimes so few that you could count them on your fingers. But it was in these humble beginnings that my passion for music deepened, unfazed by the number of fans in attendance.

Occasionally, fortune smiled upon us, and we would find ourselves playing at a youth camp. Here, in front of hundreds of people, our small stage felt like a stadium. The energy of a larger audience was electrifying, transforming these moments into monumental experiences for us. Regardless of its scale, each performance was a stepping stone, laying the foundation for the dreams we were yet to chase and, in some cases, realize.

While my brother's brilliance in engineering led him to craft computers, synthesizers, and amplifiers, I found solace in the dual realms of music and cuisine. Sports, particularly football and bandy, a unique ice sport played throughout the Nordic countries, played a significant role in my early years. However, at 16, the siren call of music proved irresistible, guiding my focus away from athletic pursuits to what would soon become my lifelong calling.

Disney Ducks and my early version of DoorDash

My entrepreneurial journey began whimsically at 17, inspired—of all things—by a Donald Duck comic. In the comic, Daisy Duck makes homemade meatballs, and Donald then delivers them to homes in their neighborhood.

It was one of those "aha" moments: I knew Sweden was ready for a similar model!

This led me to launch Sweden's pioneering fast-food delivery service in 1985; Partyservice was a venture that quickly scaled, earned a First Price from the Swedish Employers organization in their yearly competition for young entrepreneurs, and opened doors to international experiences, including a visit to the White House and IBM headquarters in the United States.

The symphony of senses

I have always believed that music and food are creative pursuits that feed the soul. They touch our deepest emotions and mirror each other in their ability to transform experiences and create profound memories. We crave different meals and different tunes on Sunday morning than we did on Saturday night.

Music is much the same. The streaming era liberated our musical choices, and I immediately fell in love.

This narrative is not just about tastes and tunes; it's about how our senses are primed by the moments we live. There are flavors that appeal to the masses, dishes that require a more refined palate, and sometimes, we need a guide to help us appreciate the nuances.

Our culinary and musical preferences evolve with our experiences, shaped by travel, new friendships, time, and discoveries.

Over time, I have realized more and more the profound similarities between these two art forms. Much like the complex layers of flavors in a well-crafted dish, music possesses the power to evoke emotions, memories, and sensations in a symphony of sound.

Just as easy-to-enjoy dishes like McDonald's burgers or spaghetti Bolognese appeal to a broad audience for their comforting familiarity, mainstream pop music often possesses an instant catchiness that allows people to easily connect with it and sing along. These are the comfort foods of the music world, offering a reliable and enjoyable experience without demanding much from the listener.

However, the true beauty of both culinary and musical exploration lies in venturing beyond the familiar.

Just as trying sushi, truffles, olives, or pâté de campagne for the first time can be a revelation, exposing oneself to new genres or artists can be equally transformative. It often requires the right environment or a moment of openness to new experiences to truly appreciate these new flavors and sounds. The memory of the first encounter with such unique tastes or melodies can leave an indelible mark, becoming a touchstone to which we return time and again for pleasure and nostalgia.

In the era of streaming, this analogy becomes even more pertinent. With virtually all the music in the world at our fingertips, our auditory palate has the potential to be as varied and rich as our culinary one. Just as we no longer limit ourselves to a single favorite dish, confining ourselves to one genre or artist in music is a thing of the past.

The digital age has democratized access to an extensive array of musical experiences, allowing us to curate the soundtrack of our lives, moment by moment, just as we might select the perfect meal to suit our mood or the occasion.

The emotional impact of music also mirrors the sensory experience of food. Much like a throwback song can transport you to the moment of your first kiss, a certain dish can evoke the warmth of a childhood kitchen or a festive family gathering. There is something profoundly powerful about how music and food can anchor us to specific times and places, triggering a cascade of memories and feelings with a single note or flavor.

I find the food analogy particularly apt in discussing music because it opens up a space for exploration and discovery. It encourages people to approach music with the curiosity and openness they might bring to trying a new cuisine.

This perspective invites listeners to expand their musical tastes, exploring new genres and artists with the same enthusiasm with which they might sample exotic dishes.

Moreover, the combination of music and food can elevate any experience, turning a simple meal into a celebration or a concert into a feast for the senses. A certain magic happens when these two elements come together, creating moments that are deeply cherished and remembered. Whether it is a jazz brunch that captures the lazy bliss of a Sunday morning or a dinner party with a playlist that perfectly complements the menu, music and food can enhance each other, enriching our lives and relationships.

In this age of endless choice and variety, our journey through the worlds of music and food is no longer about sticking to what we know. Instead, it is more about embracing the vastness of undiscovered knowledge. With each new dish we taste and every fresh track we play, we are not just consuming; we're embarking on an adventure of sensory and emotional exploration.

This journey is not just about satisfying hunger or filling silence; it is ultimately about creating a tapestry of experiences that define and enrich our existence.

I would argue that music is almost a fundamental human need, just like food. While music may not be essential for physical survival, its absence would leave an incredible void. Food and music nourish us in body and spirit–and we love to sample both of them.

In "Fan-Powered Futures," we delve further into this intricate dance by exploring how the creative arts shape our lives and communities. It's a celebration of the joy and connection these universal languages offer and a testament to their enduring power to bring us together, sparking joy and forging memories that last a lifetime.

In this evolving landscape, where every moment can be perfectly curated to our tastes, we find that music and food are not just parts of our lives but are essential threads in the global community.

A delectable duality

For nearly 15 years, I lived a life harmoniously divided between music and gastronomy and had the fortune to experience and embrace the vibrancy of both worlds.

At age 17, I embarked on an ambitious venture, launching a fast-growing food delivery service. By age 20, my business had expanded to include catering and boasted nearly 30 employees. This period of my life was marked by rapid growth and success, but it was not without its challenges.

In 1991, at the peak of my entrepreneurial journey, I faced a significant setback. Diagnosed with a chronic inflammatory bowel disease, I found myself hospitalized for nearly two years, undergoing multiple surgeries. This tested my resilience and the strength of my business. I am eternally grateful for my close friends, who stepped in during my absence to ensure the survival of my company.

Learning to live life in the present moment

This experience was also a profound wake-up call. It shattered my youthful illusion of invincibility. It further taught me to live in the moment, cherish every experience, and never take anything for granted. Interestingly, this challenging time rekindled my passion for music. I began performing more frequently, finding solace and expression through melody and lyrics.

Motivated by this renewed interest, a close friend and I co-founded Rock n' Roll Café, a rock club inspired by a previous

New York trip we had taken together where the legendary rock club with the same name at Bleecker Street blew us away.

This venture combined our love for music and food, creating a vibrant space with an open stage for bands to perform. This period remains one of the happiest and most fulfilling times of my life, a testament to the joy of pursuing one's passions.

Eventually, my partner and I pursued different paths—he ventured into nightclubs while I explored the fine dining scene. Despite this divergence, our friendship remained strong until his untimely and tragic passing, a stark reminder of life's fragility. I had the honor of playing piano and singing at his wedding; at his funeral, I was reminded yet again to live each day to the fullest and appreciate every moment.

From the highs of entrepreneurial success to the lows of personal health struggles and the loss of a dear friend, I am reminded of life's unpredictable nature. These experiences shaped me into who I am today, instilling a profound appreciation for the present and an unwavering passion for the interwoven worlds of food and music.

Finally, adversity struck one more time with a devastating fire that led to the bankruptcy of my successful fine dining restaurant. It was time to move on.

Before "American Idol" was "American Idol"

At 30, music took center stage as I formed the pop band Apple Brown Betty, achieving success in Asia and Europe with the song "Aeroplane" while securing a global record deal. This chapter led me to more songwriting and production, and I eventually signed with BMG Publishing.

Shortly after, my publisher coordinated a meeting with the one-and-only Simon Cowell, who wasn't yet a celebrity but was one of the most successful label executives at the time. Simon liked the music and wanted me to come and meet him in London.

I flew over and met Simon, who insisted, "I want you to only write songs for me and my artists." This was a massive thing in 2001 because Simon was becoming very successful in breaking new big artists.

He shared that he and Simon Fuller were debuting a new TV format called "Idol" in a few months that would give them access directly to the fans through the TV—removing the gatekeepers, who he referred to as the DJs at BBC, and who always needed to be convinced to play new records. Suddenly, we had the power to reach the fans directly. (As we all know, in just two years, "Idol" "became one of the biggest shows globally, and when "American Idol" premiered in 2002, Simon Cowell became one of the world's most famous people, if not the most liked).

I met my wife in 1998; in 2001, we had our first child, Elton. We still laugh about when I played brand-new songs over the phone through Elton's tiny Mickey Mouse boombox, which had a CD player between the ears that served as the speakers. Sometimes, I had to punch the boombox to get it back on track because it skipped so often.

Picture us: Sitting in our small apartment in Stockholm playing the latest songs on a Mickey Mouse boombox for Simon Cowell, who was in Hollywood working with "American Idol."

I had the opportunity to watch Simon's journey to becoming a mega-celebrity up close. Unfortunately for me, his focus shifted to TV over music, so It was not the big break I was hoping for, but I got the winning song for "X Factor" in the Netherlands and some other "Idol" tracks. I also had the privilege of connecting with an industry legend and having Simon as a mentor for a few years. One thing he told me still resonates.

He said, "Nick, the music industry is actually very simple. It's all about reaching the 24-year-old nurse living in the suburbs of London. If you get her, you get everything."

It was true then and remains true today.

Simon's insights on consumer understanding and brand loyalty profoundly influenced my perspective, and I'm grateful for that early connection and inspiration.

The Chipz era

During this pivotal time in my career, I had the fortune of meeting David Verdooren and Patrick van Thijn from Glam Slam. They were on the cusp of launching what would soon become one of the early 2000s' defining musical sensations: Chipz. Recognizing a shared vision and potential for groundbreaking success, they invited me to join as one of the main producers.

This partnership was the beginning of an extraordinary journey that propelled Chipz to global fame, achieving 10 worldwide number-one hits, securing 35 global top 10 chart positions, and earning numerous international awards. Our collaboration led to CD sales that reached into the millions, sell-out concerts, a successful clothing line, and even a dedicated TV show.

The band's vibrant and energetic pop music captured the hearts of countless young fans worldwide, a testament to its timeless appeal. This was highlighted decades later in 2022 when a TikTok viral trend brought Chipz's hits back into the limelight. The resurgence of our music on this global platform, captivating figures like Kim Kardashian and her daughter North West along with billions of others, underscored the enduring impact of our work.

Among the many relationships forged during this time, my friendship with David Verdooren was particularly significant. Through the highs and lows of the music industry, our bond only strengthened, and our paths would eventually converge again professionally.

David later joined me at Spotify, taking on a pivotal role as the head of the music and editorial team for the Benelux (Belgium, the Netherlands, and Luxembourg) and Germany regions. Together, we continued to shape the music industry's future, bridging our early successes with the digital revolution in music consumption.

This chapter of my life highlighted the importance of teamwork and shared goals in achieving monumental success and underscored the lasting impact of genuine friendships formed along the way.

Pirates, innovation, and "I want my MTV"

As piracy challenged the music industry, especially in the Nordic countries where Pirate Bay was located, a file-sharing platform that held all the world's music became the go-to place to find music in the mid-2000s. This rampant file sharing effectively drained the music industry in the Nordic countries, forcing major record labels to lay off much of their staff.

Ironically, this turmoil created an environment similar to Silicon Valley, one that was ripe for innovation and the birth of future music solutions that could potentially save the industry.

I firmly believe that this context significantly influenced Spotify's emergence and success. Without platforms like Pirate Bay, it is questionable whether Spotify would have obtained the test licenses needed to launch in Sweden.

The music and tech spheres were abuzz with activity as everyone sought to raise capital and gather tech talent to build a viable solution. With its early broadband penetration and rich engineering talent, Sweden became the epicenter of this transformative wave.

In my career, I continued to turn towards innovative solutions, contributing to Sweden's continued rise as a tech hub. My journey intersected with another true pro in the form of Staffan Holm of Live Nation, who became another mentor for me and has always been there for me, even bringing angel investors like Bjorn Ulveus from Abba and Per Gessle from Roxette into new ventures I created with him as an investor and chairman. A forthcoming call from Staffan changed my life.

This relationship eventually paved the way for more important partnerships and insights, particularly with Spotify and the leading Swedish telco Telia.

When I look back on these early days and influences, I can't help but think of the documentary "I Want My MTV." Like most people under 40 in that era, I was *obsessed* with MTV, which even inspired my latest company TSX—more on that later, too!

In the documentary, MTV leadership talked about how they started with a traditional broadcast model. It worked much like radio, but since it was TV, they had a camera on the DJ when he talked in between the different music videos. Even when they had a live audience in the studio, mostly for sound, MTV failed to really include them.

However, one day, "by mistake," they turned the camera to the audience, and everything changed. This is instrumental in how TV as a whole changed. The fans were now part of the show.

MTV realized that showing fans brought in a new element of emotional connection; they quickly learned that the fans are also a very important part of the format.

Later on, MTV broadcasted from beaches, colleges, and everywhere in between, pioneering this format. They also launched the first true reality show, "The Real World," which led to a huge revolution in TV that is still resonating today.

For me, the biggest takeaway from all of this was the symbiotic relationship between fans and artists, proving that "anyone" could become an influencer and celebrity and that the lines between artist and fan were blurring more with each passing day.

Answering the call of a broken industry

In 2007, the music world felt like it was on its deathbed. Especially in the Nordics, where sales were in a freefall. File-sharing sites like The Pirate Bay were the chief culprits, and the industry was scrambling for a solution.

And then, a beacon of hope arrived with the ringing of my phone. The call was from the aforementioned Staffan Holm of Live Nation, who intoned, "Your reputation precedes you. I need a consultant to evaluate an investment opportunity–maybe even a full buyout."

I could tell this wasn't just a business deal; I heard something curious and searching for more in Staffan's voice. Sweden, particularly, was in a state, with everyone from bedroom musicians to CEOs longing for *anything* to drag the music industry back from the brink.

The platform I was brought in to assess was yet another MySpace wannabe. It was clumsy and unfocused. I dove into it, analyzing it ruthlessly.

When I reported back to Staffan, there was no sugarcoating: "It has potential, but it's a mess. The organization is chaotic, and the business model treats creators as an afterthought," I told him.

It was more than just fixing some website. Standard models across the industry were based on ads, with artists seeing mere pennies on the dollar if anything at all. And that's where it clicked for me: What if we built a platform *around* the creators, a radical 50/50 split of the advertising revenue?

It was a bold premise, a MySpace killer with a conscience. Business plans and pitches to investors followed, a whirlwind where optimism battled the crushing weight of an industry in collapse.

We were not alone in this David and Goliath fight. Two other Swedish companies were on a similar path of trying to solve the future of the music industry. Soon, both Spotify and SoundCloud would emerge, and they were also initially built around an ad-supported model.

In the background, relentlessly, the team grew. The right programmers, marketers, and designers came on board, and we focused on finding those who shared the vision, even when funding hung on by a thread. Our launch goal was the end of 2008.

Snowfish's launch, when it finally happened, felt like arriving late to a party no one told us about.

Initial feedback was good; the platform itself *worked*, but that was not enough. Competing with MySpace and now the fast-growing Facebook felt insurmountable, especially with our limited resources. We needed something dramatic, and we needed it fast.

Inspiration and perspiration

Inspiration came in a flash. Talent shows were king on TV, so we wondered, "What if we harnessed that power, but did it Snowfish-style – a community-driven, online "Idol?" The power would be firmly in the hands of the audience. In late 2009, I pitched "The Next Big Thing" to Telia, the telecom giant.

They were intrigued... and they had just inked a monumental deal to bundle Spotify with their plans. Suddenly, Spotify was knocking on our door.

The negotiations stretched on painfully. A tiny startup, a telecom behemoth, and the rising star of the music world were all engaged in a three-way dance full of more missteps than graceful movement. Lawyers were everywhere, and for months, it felt like an agreement would never come. But eventually, we made it happen.

"The Next Big Thing" launched in 2010. Artists uploaded in droves, and ordinary fans signed up by the thousands to judge and guide their favorites. We did two full seasons, culminating in the second year's winner performing live at the Swedish Eurovision finals. It was both exhilarating and validating, but ultimately not *the* breakout that put Snowfish on the map.

This, however, is not a tale of defeat.

Our relationship with Telia, and crucially, with Spotify, deepened each month. By the end of 2010, Telia approached us about a problem they had noticed: finding good playlists on their bundled Spotify service was an absolute nightmare. Its generic titles and ugly URLs led to a mystery collection of songs.

What if...?

Here, in this unsexy problem, was a potential solution. I envisioned meticulous curation, playlists as works of art. But what if they were beautiful, too, like album covers from the iTunes era? What if it wasn't an algorithm doing the work but passionate fans? It felt transformative, and the team agreed.

In December, I called the team together, the energy in the room crackling. I unveiled a vision: "Think iTunes, but with playlists as the core. Imagine beautiful covers, detailed tracklists, and rich metadata. Not just for discovery, but for *organizing* music – playlists for every mood, every moment." We could give people a playlist experience akin to browsing the CD racks back when buying music felt personal.

The response was electric. "Forget the mosaic album covers Spotify uses," our lead designer exclaimed. "A playlist needs its own identity – a title, a theme, its own artwork!" Within a week, we had mockups. More than a playlist aggregator, this had the potential to be an editorial hub tied seamlessly to Spotify. This idea was so robust and different that it needed an identity.

A new company was born within our company, one with a clear focus – we decided to call it Tunigo. For the first time since launching Snowfish, that spark of hope reignited.

Tunigo's first iteration, a beta web app, launched in early 2011, intricately tied to Spotify accounts. But even from the start, we were thinking bigger. The backend was built with an API that was adaptable and could eventually work with any streaming service: Platform agnostic was the key to future growth.

Response to the beta was beyond positive. We didn't just create a tool but a community around shared music.

Then came a game-changer: Spotify announced the opening of its desktop client to third-party apps. It was definitely time to go all in. We scrambled tirelessly, transforming Tunigo into a fully-fledged desktop application. In November 2011, we proudly took our place as one of Spotify's official launch partners.

The question loomed: Will millions of Spotify users embrace something so different? The answer was a resounding *yes*.

Word spread like wildfire. Soon, Tunigo was one of the most popular apps on the platform. News outlets picked up the story and shared the human angle that went well beyond the tech story. This was about passionate fans curating music for other fans. We quickly knew that we were building something truly special.

This growth fueled new ambitions. Our editors were already creating top-notch playlists, but what if we expanded into news? Exclusive interviews? Suddenly, Tunigo was becoming a music culture authority, and landing interviews with giants like One Direction and Foster the People gave us traction far beyond our Nordic roots.

It was time to cross the Atlantic.

Doug Ford, an old friend with industry cred, was the perfect choice to lead our U.S. editorial expansion. His startup, Hit Predictor, was proof he understood the power of connecting labels with audience feedback.

Suddenly, Tunigo was not just a Nordic company; we were aiming for worldwide recognition.

But to compete globally, we needed to conquer mobile. So far, Tunigo existed only as a desktop app or within Spotify's client. Meanwhile, Spotify's free, ad-supported tier was booming on desktops, while mobile access required their premium subscription.

In June 2012, a beta Tunigo iPhone app was unleashed with a full launch on both Appstore and Android in September, pushed by strategic marketing and a wave of enthusiastic press coverage. Suddenly, we had passed the 500,000 monthly user mark, and the growth trajectory was breathtaking.

A milestone arrived in the spring of 2013: Tunigo reached the #1 spot in the Swedish App Store, even beating Spotify itself. Its validation was proof that what we had built resonated beyond our wildest dreams. We quickly climbed the ranks in the U.S. App Store's Music category, cracking the Top 10.

It was time for the next step, the one that would propel us from a cool startup to an industry titan. We needed fresh capital for rapid expansion, and now, investors were knocking on our door for the first time, not the other way around.

The most crucial attention we attracted came from Daniel Ek, the founder and CEO of Spotify, who had seen our growth and our unique approach. In 2013, that pivotal phone call would come. "Hi, it's Daniel..."

The game officially changed.

CHAPTER 2

The Playlist Revolution: Tunigo's Acquisition by Spotify

In the early '90s, I visited New York and was blown away by the new boutique hotels like Paramount Hotel with its legendary Whiskey Bar. Most of these hotels played jazzy lounge music that was just perfect–the music transformed the space into a magical, cool environment that made you never want to leave.

I remember thinking how incredibly powerful music is and that the right music at the right moment and the right place really can change the whole experience. That really impacted my journey with both Tunigo and Spotify.

Tunigo quickly became a Spotify partner. When Spotify launched, it was all about the magic that every song was available at your fingertips, but you needed to know what you wanted to listen to, and you either created your own playlist or had a friend who did great "mixtapes" do it and share the playlist with you. If you shared a playlist with someone, it came as a long, clunky link without a name, a description, or anything of value.

Tunigo made it easy—and fun—to find, create, and share new music and playlists on Spotify and was pretty much an instant hit: Tunigo was a top 10 app on Spotify from the first day it launched its app platform, not to mention a top contender in global music categories on the Apple App Store (it even outperformed Spotify in the Swedish App Store).

My Spotify origin story

Three years later, I was skiing and enjoying a little family time when I received a call that would change my life. Spotify CEO and co-founder Daniel Ek expressed an interest in us meeting. When I arrived and saw both Daniel and co-founder Martin Lorentzon in the room, I immediately thought, "They want to buy us."

However, they proceeded to ask about Tunigo's progress and fundraising, with no discussion of an acquisition or further partnership. I left the meeting puzzled but still anticipating something more.

A couple of hours later, I received the call I knew was coming: Daniel wanted to set up another meeting.

At our second meeting, Martin made that game-changing offer, sharing, "We want to buy your company and make it part of Spotify."

Martin looked up from his phone, stated the price they were willing to pay, and went back to scrolling. Many months later, that is exactly what we agreed upon.

Nevertheless, I was thrilled. I could tell that Daniel and Martin had a real vision for integrating Tunigo within Spotify and entrusting me with the task of building out Spotify playlists globally while forming a substantial global programming and editorial team.

The night before the acquisition was set to close, I received a call at 1 a.m., a time when no good news, other than potentially the birth of a baby, comes. There were concerns over Tunigo's open-source coding.

After three hours and a lot of wrangling, including talking to experts in Silicon Valley to get confirmation that the code was not a problem, the deal was finally signed. I prepared a statement for the media that shared my obvious excitement over the news, and I thought that was that.

Little did I know that I would have to leave a Bruce Springsteen concert in Stockholm that night when I was hit up by a barrage of calls, texts, and emails from what felt like every reporter in the world.

The floodgates had opened, and it was clear that we were not the only ones who thought this was really big news.

Data and discovery

This marked the birth of "Spotify Playlists. Redefined Music," and Spotify transformed into a true powerhouse for artist discovery. Our unique playlist syndicate setup allowed new artists to climb from feeder playlists to the flagship of Today's Top Hits, turning mixtape artists into global superstars.

My kids' Instagram feeds were suddenly filled with new artists begging them for some Spotify love, and our building's package rooms were brimming with gold records with our names engraved on them. The playlist revolution continued to roll, and the industry continued to change on a dime.

Sure, it was about creativity and innovation. But the biggest shift was all about data. Believe me, it is a lot sexier than it sounds.

We wanted to know everything about performance. How long were songs listened to? Which ones were saved? Which ones were shared?

We introduced an online portal for music submission, allowing us to "decorate" new tracks with various attributes including genre, popularity, social following, and previous playlist inclusions. This system also categorized artists into tiers based on their monthly listeners, ensuring that each artist was appropriately placed within our ecosystem.

Songs could ascend through our system based on their performance in feeder playlists, which were tailored to specific moments and genres. A track's journey could begin in lower-tier playlists and, if the data supported it, progress to flagship playlists, with the ultimate goal of being featured in Today's Top Hits, the number one playlist on our service.

Machine learning tools enhanced our system even further, allowing us to attribute tracks accurately and integrate them into personalized algorithmic playlists. This scalability meant that more songs could receive the exposure they deserved.

The industry went from a model where the gut feelings of a few execs led the way to a metrics-driven world. Our rock-solid process was backed by data at every step. We had rules. We had protocols. (My kids did not make anyone famous on Instagram, Spotify, or otherwise, and we didn't take any bribes.) And we had the data to prove why it was working.

The rise of music curation

The old music world was one of ownership. Your record collection was more than personal entertainment; it was also a badge of identity. Each album, carefully purchased – often with limited pocket money – represented a deliberate choice, a statement of taste. There was a tangible pride in building that sonic library, each vinyl sleeve a brick in the wall of "you."

Money was the gatekeeper, deciding not just what you could listen to but how deeply you could explore your favorite songs and sounds. The streaming revolution shattered these boundaries. Suddenly, the world's sonic tapestry lay at your fingertips.

This all-access pass was a double-edged sword. It liberated listeners from financial constraints, letting them sample music with the gluttony of a kid in a candy store. Yet, it also sparked an overwhelming sense of "Where do I even begin?"

The paradox of unlimited choice became a new barrier.

This was the epiphany that fueled my journey. Recognizing the industry-wide shift from ownership to engagement, I saw a desperate need for curation.

No longer was it a statement to simply like an artist – anyone could now access anyone. The new statement revolved more around discovery, navigating the endless stream to find the perfect soundtrack for each moment.

Inspired by how we approach food, tuned to mood and occasion, I envisioned a world where music followed life's rhythms. This was the heart of Tunigo, a platform designed to bridge the gap in the all-access model.

Tunigo wasn't just about playlists. It was about crafting musical experiences.

Our curators delved into genres, but more importantly, they dug into moods and situations. They built sonic journeys specifically designed for heartbreak or house parties, lazy Sunday mornings, or the focused energy of a workday hustle.

The goal was simple: to gift listeners the perfect soundtrack for any moment, curated with expertise and soul. In this newly boundless world of music, the mission wasn't to sell tracks—it was to turn listening into an effortless, joyful exploration. We aimed to be the guides on a grand sonic adventure, ensuring that, in this era of choice overload, the perfect song was always just a click away.

"That's the way it has always been done" was no longer the way it was being done.

All of this change freaked a lot of people out. Especially the people who preferred "the way it's always been done."

For the first time, the music industry wasn't about who you knew. It was no longer a boys' club ruled by the exclusive few.

The music industry was *finally* a meritocracy. We truly needed a system that championed meritocracy – where the quality and appeal of the music, rather than industry politics, dictated its success.

This merit-based system revolutionized how we discovered and promoted talent. It allowed us to identify and elevate artists based *solely* on fan reactions and the data that supported it, transforming mixtape artists into superstars who could headline sold-out tours. Our platform became a launchpad for new talent, democratizing music discovery in an unprecedented way.

Spotify's model was revolutionary at the time: streaming music legally, with the consent of artists and labels. It was a bold move, balancing the tightrope between the industry's demands and the consumer's needs.

Once resistant to online models, the industry began to realize that digital distribution was inevitable and potentially lucrative.

In Sweden, this period fostered a unique ecosystem where tech innovation intersected with the creative arts. The country's history of strong music exports and a robust tech sector created the perfect breeding ground for the next generation of music services. It was a confluence of necessity, opportunity, and talent– factors that rarely align so perfectly.

CHAPTER 3

At the Helm of a Revolution: Leading Spotify's Global Music Domination

It was finally time for the revolution...

In May 2013, following the acquisition of Tunigo by Spotify, our team continued to operate out of our Stockholm office, preparing for the transition into Spotify's headquarters. We balanced the excitement of joining a global leader in music streaming with the practicalities of integrating two distinct corporate cultures and operational systems. It was equally exciting and exhausting.

Tunigo's presence was not limited to Stockholm; our footprint extended across the Atlantic to Saratoga, New York. Despite this global reach, the two years leading up to the acquisition were riddled with a series of financial challenges. On multiple occasions, we found ourselves teetering on the brink of bankruptcy. Yet, through sheer determination and strategic maneuvering, we managed to stay afloat.

A critical partnership at a critical time

One of the pivotal moments in our pre-acquisition phase involved securing critical capital to meet payroll obligations. Our solution came in the form of a partnership with Telia, a major Swedish telecommunications company.

I vividly recall the supportive wishes from the rest of the team as I set out for Telia's headquarters on a mission to secure a solution for our immediate need for funds to cover the upcoming payroll. My fervent wishes were granted.

The deal was structured uniquely: Telia would fund a marketing campaign and a crucial cash advance to Tunigo. In return, Telia would be entitled to a percentage of the sale proceeds if Tunigo were to be acquired within a two-year period. This investment was a true gamble on their part, banking on the potential of our company's future success.

Little did we know at the time that this move would lead to a fruitful outcome for Telia following our acquisition by Spotify. I am still incredibly grateful to the amazing people at Telia– Mats Alpberg, Lars Roth, and Fredrik Brunzell–who believed in this vision during some challenging times.

This partnership came at a critical juncture for both Tunigo and Spotify and served as a bridge to our later successes.

A more-than-memorable transition to Spotify HQ

The day we walked into Spotify's headquarters in Stockholm was one of the most powerful moments of my career.

Picture this: The moment our team of 18 from Tunigo stepped into the Spotify office for the first time post-acquisition, we were awestruck. It dawned on us that we were now part of this vast, vibrant green machine boasting the most impressive office space we had ever seen.

Everywhere we looked, there were fully stocked fridges, gaming rooms, and state-of-the-art technology. Greetings poured in from various teams as we made our way to the boardroom. There, Daniel greeted us with a warm welcome, flanked by rows of champagne bottles. It was a moment of pure celebration, marking our official integration into Spotify.

This shift, this growth, and this opportunity symbolized the culmination of our journey through turbulence and uncertainty to the epicenter of the music industry's most groundbreaking company.

Visionary beats: Spotify's leap to 500 million users

Joining Spotify in 2013 was a pivotal moment in my career, placing me at the heart of a rapidly evolving music industry. At the time, Spotify was a burgeoning platform with around 6 million paying subscribers out of a total of 24 million users, straddling the line between startup energy and global influence.

However, the real story began in the summer of 2013, during a significant global gathering in Stockholm that brought together employees from across the world. The theme of this summer event was "500 million users," a target that, at the time, seemed not just ambitious but almost fantastical.

I remember the buzz of excitement and the undercurrent of skepticism as we all tried to wrap our heads around this number. What did our CEO mean by setting such a seemingly unattainable goal? Over those four days, discussions and debates swirled around the potential strategies and implications of such an aspiration. It wasn't just about the numerical goal; it was the audacity of the vision that sparked conversations, challenging our perceptions of what was possible.

Reflecting on those days from the perspective of March 2024, with Spotify now boasting over 600 million users, more than

220 million of them paying subscribers, the impact of setting such a bold goal is undeniable. This phenomenal growth underscores the power of manifesting ambitious goals and the importance of visionary leadership in the entrepreneurial journey.

Being part of Spotify's journey from those early days of ambitious targets to the current reality, where those once lofty goals have been surpassed, has been nothing short of inspiring. It taught me the critical lesson that to achieve extraordinary results, one must dare to dream big, setting sights on horizons that seem beyond reach. This mindset is what differentiates successful entrepreneurs and leaders from the rest: the courage to set bold, seemingly unrealistic goals and the tenacity to work relentlessly toward making them a reality.

The transformation of Spotify from a promising startup to a global powerhouse in the music streaming industry exemplifies how clear, bold visions can materialize into tangible achievements. Daniel Ek's leadership and his ability to manifest such a goal into reality have propelled Spotify to new heights and redefined the music industry's landscape.

This journey of exponential growth and the realization of a once-unimaginable goal illustrate the essence of entrepreneurship: the blend of bold vision and steadfast perseverance. For any entrepreneur or business leader, the lesson is clear—embrace audacity, maintain a firm belief in your vision, and never yield in the face of skepticism or obstacles.

Witnessing Spotify's rise and participating in its evolution has been a testament to the power of goal manifestation. It's a narrative that emphasizes the importance of setting ambitious targets and fostering a culture that relentlessly pursues them. Daniel and Spotify's story is not just about numbers and market shares; it's about envisioning the future of an industry and relentlessly pushing the boundaries to redefine what's achievable.

In the broader context of "Fan-Powered Futures," this story of Spotify's ambitious goal and realization serves as a powerful narrative thread, illustrating the transformative impact of visionary leadership and bold entrepreneurial spirit in the digital age. As we explore the dynamic interplay between fans, artists, and the platforms that connect them, the saga of Spotify's meteoric rise offers valuable insights into the potential of clear, ambitious goals to drive unprecedented growth and change.

Thus, Spotify's journey is not just a business success story; it's a beacon for innovators and dreamers worldwide, proving that with bold vision and unwavering commitment, even the most audacious goals are within reach. In the ever-evolving landscape of music and technology, such stories are essential, inspiring a new generation of entrepreneurs to dream big and push forward.

Playlists bigger than the biggest radio station

Spotify CEO Daniel Ek had a clear vision for our integration. He initially wanted Tunigo to maintain its independence, allowing us to establish our footing before gradually merging our engineering, product, and design teams into Spotify's broader ecosystem.

Our biggest contribution to this acquisition? Spotify's own playlists.

Until we joined forces, Spotify had not ventured into creating its own curated playlists. This changed in 2013 with the launch of the "Browse" feature and Spotify playlists. When I joined Spotify, I told Daniel, "Playlists could be bigger than the biggest radio station." Together, we later proved this to be true.

This innovation allowed users to navigate through categories, discovering the perfect playlist for any moment and any experience. Spotify playlists, which are now a cornerstone of the platform's user experience, were a direct result of the Tunigo acquisition–and one of the things I am most proud of bringing to the table.

It was the start of turning consumers into fans.

Global expansion and innovation: Focus, focus, focus

It was time to broaden our editorial horizons by amplifying Spotify's global editorial presence.

Understanding the significance of local music and the need to curate music for every imaginable moment, we embarked on a mission to hire editorial leads globally. This expansion would be on a worldwide scale. We soon had editorial leads in various countries, each building out their local teams and bringing their unique cultural and musical insights to the table.

And then we went to Iceland…

Iceland is home to active volcanoes, beautiful landscape, the legendary hot springs, and the potential for a lot of innovation and creativity.

Our first global offsite in Iceland turned into an international hit. Gustav Söderström, the Chief Product Officer for Spotify, presented us with an audacious challenge: *create a new category in the Browse feature and launch it within two hours.*

You heard that right: two hours! Creating a brand-new category was one (big) thing. Launching it that fast was a whole other challenge.

In a flurry, teams scrambled to brainstorm ideas, design icons, and curate images for categories and playlist covers. The atmosphere was electric, charged with our global team's collective energy and passion. Miraculously, within the two-hour deadline, we conceptualized and executed the launch of a new category called "FOCUS."

The FOCUS category was an instant hit, resonating profoundly with our users. Playlists like Peaceful Piano, Intensive Studying, Namaste, and Deep Focus seemingly amassed millions of followers overnight. In particular, Peaceful Piano, curated by Meg Tarquino, became a standout success, attracting over 8 million followers and gaining more listeners every day. All of this from one offsite in Iceland: It was a testament to teamwork and some pretty bright and curious minds coming together.

This success wasn't just a matter of numbers—it also validated our approach to user experience. By carefully crafting images, titles, and descriptions, we set clear expectations for our users, priming them for the experience they sought. These playlists didn't just provide music; they enhanced focus and productivity, aligning perfectly with their intended purpose. They were purposeful and powerful—and don't forget popular!

We were clearly meeting our fans' needs–and we were clearly creating true fans. They were tuning in and staying tuned in. We were not just a platform for music discovery and enjoyment–we were a real and integral part of our users' daily lives, helping them focus, relax, and be more productive (not to mention have more fun). This achievement underlined the power of understanding and catering to the nuanced demands of our global audience.

Spotify's mission, "to connect as many artists as possible with as many fans as possible," was a clarion call that heralded the dawn of a new era in the music industry. This vision, powered by the relentless forces of data and innovation, catalyzed a complete transformation from a retail-centric model to one of seamless access. It was a bold departure from the traditional norms where only about 25% of music listeners actively engaged with record stores, with the majority relying on radio and television for their musical diet, perhaps purchasing a solitary record during festive seasons.

Teamwork makes the dream work

With its diverse and dynamic musical landscape, the U.S. market was identified as a critical area for expansion. Here, genres like Hip Hop, Country, and Latin music reigned supreme.

Recognizing this, Doug Ford and I embarked on a mission to assemble a world-class team. Our goal was to cover every significant musical style, including mood and moment playlists, catering to a wide array of listener preferences. Clearly, it was no small goal.

The genre leads we recruited were game-changers. Our first major hire was Tuma Basa, who would go on to create the dynamic RapCaviar brand, a name that today stands as a benchmark in the Hip Hop industry. Tuma, who was then working at Diddy's Revolt Music, brought an unparalleled depth of understanding and vision. Joining him were Mjeema Picket, heading RnB and Soul, and Austin Kramer, leading Dance Music. Their combined expertise set us on an exciting trajectory.

The momentum continued with the addition of Mike Biggane, whose innovative approach led to creating iconic brands within the Pop music genre, notably Today's Top Hits and New Music Friday. Roccio Guerrero, as the Latin lead, played a pivotal role in launching Viva Latino, a brand that significantly boosted Spotify's presence in the Latin music market. The addition of Alison Hagendorf for Rock and John Marks for Country completed what we fondly referred to as our dream team.

This team of pros laid the foundation for iconic brands like RapCaviar, Today's Top Hits, New Music Friday, Viva Latino, Hot Country, and Rock this. It was a dream team and then some.

With these notable successes under our belt, a new era dawned at Spotify.

Our next objective was twofold: 1) to revolutionize the way new artists were introduced and 2) to connect an ever-growing audience to new music.

Turning the page to a new chapter in music streaming and hip hop's rise to dominance

This assembly of experts marked just the beginning of a new chapter in music streaming. The impact was profound: Not only did we succeed in breaking new artists and connecting fans to new music, but we also established Spotify as a global leader in music curation across diverse genres and styles.

The success of this strategy was evident in how these curated playlists and genre-specific programs resonated with listeners. Spotify had transformed from a platform that merely hosted music to an influential force in shaping musical tastes and trends.

The music industry's tectonic shift towards streaming was much more than just a technological switch—it was a cultural earthquake.

Before, the path for aspiring artists was narrow and heavily guarded. You needed expensive studio time to produce professional-quality music. Then, you had to convince record labels and radio stations—the gatekeepers of the era—that your sound was worth playing. It was a system built on exclusivity, often limited by personal taste and genre prejudice.

Hip hop faced this uphill battle head-on. Despite its grassroots popularity, much of mainstream radio refused to embrace the raw, rhythmic, often socially conscious sound of hip hop. But technology has a way of sidestepping those in power.

The rise of accessible music production software and democratic distribution on streaming services turned the tables.

No longer were recording budgets and gatekeepers the deciding factors in reaching an audience, and hip hop enjoyed this sea change in a big way.

This seismic change in the industry birthed a generation of hip hop superstars. Artists like Drake, J. Cole, and Kendrick Lamar honed their craft in bedrooms and basements, building loyal online followings before ever setting foot in a traditional studio. Their music, unfiltered by label executives or radio programmers, resonated with an audience hungry for authenticity. Chance the Rapper, a pioneer of independent success, famously bypassed the record label system entirely, achieving widespread acclaim without ever signing a traditional deal.

Suddenly, young artists could craft entire tracks on laptops, uploading them directly to the masses. This sonic revolution fueled an explosion of fresh hip hop sounds. The genre, once held back by traditional barriers, surged forward with diverse voices and new perspectives. The audience, now empowered with unlimited choice, responded in force.

Streaming didn't just make hip hop accessible; it turned listeners into explorers. Instead of a handful of radio hits, they could dive into the genre's rich history and its endless sub-genres. Playlists and algorithms helped people discover the conscious lyricism of earlier acts like A Tribe Called Quest or the infectious trap beats of artists like Migos and Future.

This shift is a potent example of fans and technology joining forces. They took the power from those who had long been the tastemakers and placed it into the hands—and ears—of the people.

No longer limited by top-down decisions and commercial biases, the audience became the ultimate arbiter of success. And they chose hip hop, fueling its meteoric rise to the top of the musical charts and the hearts of listeners worldwide.

The celebrity collaborations you're dying to know more about

In 2015, our journey at Spotify took a leap into uncharted territory. Following the success of our new Browse categories, we joined forces with the product team to curate unique musical experiences.

Our ambition led to creating the Running App, a feature that revolutionized how people interacted with music during their workouts. Using cutting-edge technology, we ensured that the tempo of the music matched the runner's pace. This required artists to produce various mixes of their tracks at different tempos, allowing the app to synchronize the music with the runner's stride. "Running Originals" was born out of this innovative idea, with Tiesto, the iconic Dutch DJ. He was the perfect first artist to create dedicated tracks for this feature.

This new feature led us to DJ Khaled. At the time, he was a well-known DJ and curator in Miami but had not yet achieved widespread fame. Tuma Basa, our Hip Hop lead, saw potential in Khaled for creating content for the Running App.

My first interaction with Khaled was via a Zoom call, and his charisma was immediately palpable–even across the screen and across the miles. I realized then that we needed to do something more significant with him to capture his vibrant personality in a visual format.

Tuma and I flew to Miami to meet DJ Khaled in his studio. At that time, Spotify did not feature *any* video content, so this was a groundbreaking initiative. Our internal video team, primarily focused on promotional and commercial content, was tasked with a new challenge.

Meeting Khaled in person confirmed my belief that we should create a series of original videos featuring him, so we hired Adam Soldingar as the new Head of Editorial Video and embarked on producing "The Key to Success" videos with Khaled.

However, during the production of these original videos, Khaled released a Snapchat video that went viral, depicting him getting lost on his jet ski in Miami. This moment catapulted him to celebrity status and worldwide fame and simultaneously popularized Snapchat. Within weeks, Khaled's career skyrocketed, leading to a record deal with Epic Records.

Looking back, I realized we were onto something big with Khaled. Although the timing wasn't perfect, this endeavor propelled us into the realm of video content and laid the groundwork for developing new features that would push the music industry into its next evolutionary phase.

The rise of vertical video

During this period, most video content was in the 16:9 horizontal format. However, apps like Snapchat were pioneering the use of vertical videos, which felt more personal and intimate, akin to a FaceTime call. This inspired us to advocate for a new vertical format for music videos on Spotify.

Our data indicated that younger audiences rarely rotated their phones and wanted to engage with content in vertical mode. We envisioned a format that wasn't necessarily high-budget but could be as simple as a one-shot video filmed on a mobile phone, creating a complete and more intimate experience for fans.

Vertical videos rapidly gained traction in the industry, capturing the interest of artists who found this novel mode of expression both intimate and refreshing. Its simplicity and cost-effectiveness made it an appealing alternative to traditionally expensive music video productions.

We were never trying to compete with the music video industry, but vertical videos were a newer, more personal way for artists to connect with fans. I felt strongly that we were underutilizing the "now playing" view – the canvas of our app – and that it held untapped potential for deeper storytelling.

Our product team developed the capability to interweave vertical videos into playlists and included the option for storytelling, enhancing the narrative and connection between artists and their music. Storytelling would turn out to be a big deal for both Spotify and the industry as a whole.

Presenting this new format to record labels met with a mix of skepticism and curiosity. A significant breakthrough came when Interscope Records chairman and CEO John Janick, recognizing the potential of this format, convinced Selena Gomez to participate.

With the single "Bad Liar," Selena Gomez became the first artist to use this feature. She really embraced the format and took it even one step further when she released the second vertical video for the song "Wolves" featuring Marshmello. That video starts out with a FaceTime call between Selena and Marshmello, and after that, she filmed herself using her iPhone as "one take" while walking around her house.

The song was a massive success and has today been streamed more than 1.5 billion times on Spotify alone. This moment marked the birth of a new and engaging format that placed artists at the forefront and offered fans a unique view and experience.

As vertical video gained traction, Spotify introduced the Canvas feature – a lower-touch version where artists could upload short videos looped during song playback. This innovation enriched the listening experience even more, allowing artists to visually represent their songs and connect with listeners in a novel way.

We also started to incorporate vertical videos into our flagship playlists. This move was more than just a visual enhancement–it was about weaving the stories behind the songs and, yes, creating even more connections.

Looking back, I believe continued investment in in-client video support and fan interactions could have further revolutionized music discovery on Spotify. If artists could communicate directly with their fans in the Spotify app, the landscape of music discovery might have been different today, potentially challenging platforms like TikTok in their dominance.

Making waves in the United States

Despite what the landscape looks like today, it was not exactly an easy start for Spotify in the United States.

Our interactions with label executives and artists were often humbling. Back then, Spotify was perceived as a cool, albeit small, startup in the vast ocean of the music industry. This perception significantly influenced our negotiations and collaborations.

Label executives would often remark, "You are such a small part of our revenue," which really encapsulated the challenge we faced in securing commitments.

In 2016, however, the shift we had been pushing for finally happened as the music industry recognized our growing influence in the United States. No longer were we just a novel startup; Spotify was starting to carve out a notable role in the music streaming landscape, and the music industry realized that we were an important partner for breaking artists and a strong catalyst for revenue and profits.

This was suddenly clear when it came to our dealings with labels and artists. The conversations changed. The expressions changed. The interest changed. We were met with a newfound eagerness and interest in potential partnerships and collaborations.

The rise of The Weeknd

One 2016 meeting really stands out for me.

Republic Records, under the leadership of CEO and Chairman Monte Lipman, came to our office with Wassim "Sal" Slaiby, representing Abel Tesfaye, better known as The Weeknd, who was well on his way to global stardom.

At this time, The Weeknd had already tasted success with his "Beauty Behind The Madness" album and was on the verge of releasing "Starboy." Sal, who was fully charged and focused on immediate sales, initially showed little interest in our proposal for a more sustainable, long-term strategy centered around our playlist system. Our vision was clear: We wanted to elevate The Weeknd to a global superstar level, something we firmly believed our playlists and programming strategy could achieve.

This memorable meeting, facilitated by Troy Carter, head of Creator Services at Spotify, was intense—think sharp exchanges and high emotions from start to finish. Despite the initial resistance, with Monte's considerable support, we gradually steered the conversation towards a mutual agreement, not to mention what was to become a global phenomenon.

"Starboy," the album's lead single featuring the iconic French duo Daft Punk, was clearly going to be a hit. This one track became the testbed for our strategy. As history shows, our approach was not just successful but groundbreaking. Abel, Sal, and Monte were astounded by the results. The album soared, marking a monumental success globally and solidifying The Weeknd as one of the planet's biggest artists.

"Starboy" topped the charts in the United States, Canada, France, the Netherlands, New Zealand, and my home country of Sweden. It was The Weeknd's fourth number-one single and

Daft Punk's first. It later won "Best Urban Contemporary Album" at the 60th Annual Grammy Awards.

Fast forward eight years to January 2024, and "Starboy" has been streamed over 3 billion times on Spotify alone. It remains a Top 50 track on the Global Chart, and The Weeknd is the #1 most-played artist on Spotify.

The relationship I forged with Sal and Monte in that memorable meeting has endured, evolving into a lifelong friendship. We often reminisce about that day, acknowledging its significance in all of our careers and, more importantly, in the meteoric rise of Abel.

It was a pivotal moment that underscored the power of strategic collaboration, the importance of fans, and the role of Spotify in reshaping the music landscape.

The Chateau Marmont Grammy Watch Party

One of the most memorable events that year was our Grammy watch party. Hosted in Bungalow 1 at the legendary Chateau Marmont in West Hollywood, the event was a testament to our burgeoning status. And we were excited to be there.

Despite the prestigious location, Spotify still struggled to attract guests. Though modest in scale, this event of about 30 movers and shakers represented our initial steps in aligning with the grandeur of the music industry's most illustrious events. In case you're curious, Kendrick Lamar won the most trophies (five) that year, and Taylor Swift won three, including her first Album of the Year–she was the first female artist to bring that bigtime award home.

The following year, 2017, marked a more dramatic change. We hosted our first Grammy Party at The Balasco Theatre in Los Angeles for the Best New Artist category, featuring performances by The Chainsmokers and Maren Morris, among others. This event was a stark contrast to the previous year's watch party. It was a grand affair, reflecting Spotify's newly elevated status in the industry.

The Best New Artist Party quickly became the most coveted ticket during Grammy Week, symbolizing our arrival on the big stage and even more shifts in the music industry.

These events were truly more than just parties; they were milestones in Spotify's journey in the U.S. music industry. From a start-up seeking validation to hosting one of the most sought-after events during Grammy Week, our journey was all about perseverance, innovation, and the power of music to connect people. It was a revolution.

This ascendancy marked Spotify's growing influence and underscored the shifting dynamics in the music streaming industry, with Spotify at the forefront of this revolution.

We learned about true fandom firsthand and witnessed the power of putting music in the people's hands.

RapCaviar: The Tour

As 2017 drew to a close, Spotify's flagship brands, RapCaviar and Viva Latino, had evolved into authoritative voices in their respective genres. Recognizing their influence, we embarked on an ambitious project to bring these virtual experiences into the real world, connecting artists and fans in a tangible, unforgettable way.

RapCaviar, under the innovative leadership of Tuma Basa, took a groundbreaking step by going on tour. The concept was unique: to take the brand across various cities, each a cornerstone in the history of Hip Hop, and ensure that the headline artists were local to those cities. This approach not only celebrated the roots of Hip Hop but also paid homage to the local talents who shaped its journey.

The tour was a resounding success, with each event selling out rapidly. Some concerts drew such massive crowds that they necessitated police intervention for crowd control. This phenomenon was a testament to the cultural resonance and impact of RapCaviar.

Inspired by the success of RapCaviar, we replicated this model with Viva Latino. The objective was the same: to forge a real-life connection between artists and their fans, celebrating the vibrancy and diversity of Latin music.

The defining moment for RapCaviar and its cultural significance came with the inception of the RapCaviar Pantheon. At the end of the year, we celebrated the three biggest artists in a unique, grand fashion by creating a modern rendition of the "Pantheon," exhibiting life-sized sculptures of each artist at the Brooklyn Museum. These sculptures were a marvel of technology and art, crafted by state-of-the-art robotic arms from 3D scans of the artists. Fans could follow the creation process online, engaging in speculation and anticipation about the identities of the honored artists. They were invested well before the main event.

Upon reflection, these initiatives were more than just events or exhibitions; they were cultural movements. They bridged the gap between the digital and physical worlds, bringing to life the music fans adored in a format they could experience and interact with. It was a bold statement that Spotify was not just a part of the music industry but also a driving force shaping its future.

CHAPTER 4

A Year with Drake and Lady Gaga That Changed Everything

It feels like 2018 was the year when *everything happened*. From the Grammys to the Drakeover to "A Star is Born," it was an epic year in music history and maybe an even more epic year in my life.

The year kicked off with one of the biggest Grammy parties ever seen or imagined. To celebrate the Grammy's 60th anniversary, the awards show was broadcast live from Madison Square Garden in the Big Apple–the date was moved to January to avoid conflict with the Winter Olympics.

Spotify went ALL IN. We hosted a new artist Grammy pre-party featuring Khalid, SZA, Lili Uzi Vert, Julia Michaels, and Alessia Cara, plus a surprise cameo from Logic with his Grammy-nominated hit "1-800-273-8255" and an unexpected appearance by Marshmello.

Crazy lines. Celebrities. Dancing and singing and partying. Epic from start to finish.

In my mind, this was when everyone realized Spotify was the dominant number-one player in the music industry. "Massive" doesn't do this event justice–it was an unbelievable night of the best new music from the leading player in the industry.

And that was just the beginning of the year that changed everything.

Time for a global shift

In April, Spotify went public on the New York Stock Exchange through a direct listing rather than a traditional IPO–pioneering the direct listing in our own innovative way. It was transparent and leveled the playing field for investors. Spotify opened at an impressive $165.90–a market value of $29.5 billion. Not bad for a day at the office. This elevated our status and opened the floodgates of requests for partnerships and collaborations.

Amidst all this, I moved to New York–a big shift for me, my family, and my work. As the new Global Head of Music for Spotify, it only made sense to come to the epicenter of the industry. A bigger role meant more responsibilities, more pressure–and more opportunities.

Relocating to New York with my family marked a significant transition that opened up a realm of opportunities. In my new role, it was imperative for me to be at the heart of the industry.

With numerous team members based in New York, proximity to my team and the epicenter of business significantly simplified professional and personal logistics. After spending almost half of the previous year traveling and meandering through too many time zones to count, it was time to settle down and reunite with my family.

This move also presented a timely opportunity for our teenage children to immerse themselves in a new culture and environment. Elton, previously attending a music high school in Sweden, and Enni, on the cusp of her high school journey, were at pivotal stages in their lives. Our exploratory visit to New York emphasized the importance of education in our decision-making process. Ultimately, we settled in a quaint village in Westchester, chosen for its renowned public schools. The schools' resemblance to those seen in American high school movies, which were very familiar to the kids from Swedish television, was an added bonus that eased the transition.

I did not take this decision to move across continents lightly, but the choice was ultimately met with unanimous excitement from the entire family. The prospect of starting anew in New York, a city that promised enrichment and growth in countless ways, was thrilling.

As we embarked on this adventure across the Atlantic, it was with a collective sense of anticipation and eagerness for the experiences ahead.

You may have heard of the Drakeover…

Spotify and Apple Music had been going head to head for a while, with Apple Music demanding artist exclusives. And they initially got some big ones–including Taylor Swift and Drake at one time.

While exclusives might have initially made sense from a financial vantage point, when my pre-teen said she didn't want a box of Taylor Swift merchandise that showed up at our home in Stockholm shortly before our move because "I don't really know who she is," it was clear that artists were giving up a huge part of their fanbase in Europe if they did not choose to come to Spotify.

When it came to Drake and Spotify, we decided to go all in for the release of his "Scorpion" album. We determined that all attention was good attention and that we needed to prove our prowess to the industry even more than consumers at that moment.

So we put Drake EVERYWHERE in the Spotify app to create a true pop culture moment–and it worked. We had received more than 50 exclusive Drake photos from the management that popped up on playlists (including many that didn't include a single Drake song). It was hard-core publicity at its best, and it broke every record, becoming the fastest album ever to reach 1 billion streams worldwide.

The press dubbed this all-out promotion blitz the "Drakeover" to describe the intense promotional campaign, which, admittedly, may have saturated the Spotify interface with more Drake content than some users appreciated. This event was a big move for the industry and ended all discussion around "exclusives" while demonstrating the transformative potential of fully utilizing our platform's capabilities.

The aftermath left no doubt: Spotify had emerged as the paramount ally for artists and record labels alike. Furthermore, this episode highlighted the formidable influence of fans in driving change within the expansive music industry.

"A Star is Born" and then some

Our meetings with Lady Gaga later that year didn't exactly start out on the right foot.

Lady Gaga's 2016 return with "Perfect Illusion," the first single off her "Joanne" album, marked a pivotal moment. It was her first major solo release since 2009, a gap during which the industry had undergone a seismic shift toward streaming. Spotify's audience skewed younger, and many listeners were unfamiliar with Gaga's earlier work. Her new sound also contrasted with the dominant pop trends of the time.

Recognizing these challenges, we argued against immediate top-tier playlist placement for "Perfect Illusion." The landscape was hyper-competitive, and we feared the song might flounder, hurting its long-term potential with unfamiliar listeners. Instead, we proposed a gradual build-up strategy, better suited for introducing legacy artists to a new generation.

Lady Gaga's label and management initially pushed for prime placement in Today's Top Hits. We compromised with a slightly lower position. Our prediction ultimately proved correct – in the cutthroat playlist environment, the song's high skip rate eventually caused it to slide.

This experience fostered a turning point. The label and management gained a deeper understanding of how our system works and leaned on us more for strategic advice. It fueled a strong partnership moving forward, focused on tailoring music introduction strategies for established artists seeking to connect with younger audiences in the streaming age. This led to a greater understanding on both sides about collaborating effectively in the ever-evolving music landscape.

However, when John Janick from Interscope reached out about Lady Gaga's upcoming album for the movie "A Star is Born," our team was absolutely blown away after a private viewing. We immediately recognized the potential of the movie and the beautiful old-school soundtrack. It was the same artist two years later with profoundly different results. Not only is "Shallow" the most streamed Lady Gaga song, but it also won her an Oscar for Best Original Song in 2019.

All of these events spotlight Spotify's role as a mirror of public taste, where any song or artist could rise to the top based on merit. "A Star is Born" and "Shallow" proved that traditional notions of what constitutes a "hit" were changing.

In 2018, my life transformed both professionally and personally.

Spotify solidified its position as a leader in the music industry, driving forward the concept of music as a meritocracy. It was a year of new beginnings in New York, witnessing firsthand the power of music to connect, transform, and transcend boundaries.

As the year came to a close, I was starting to ask myself: "What's next?"

CHAPTER 5

What Came Next: Times Square-Style Entertainment

As the calendar turned to 2019, it heralded not just another year but a new milestone. The Spotify Music squad was bound for Cancun, Mexico, poised for a grand global music symposium. The event gathered nearly 400 professionals from across the globe who converged in Mexico for this star-studded summit.

The conference teemed with distinguished guest speakers, including the likes of hailed record and ad executive Steve Stoute. But the crowning moment was an electrifying performance by Latin music icon Nicky Jam, etching this event as a pinnacle moment in my career journey and Spotify's global prominence.

Looking back and moving forward

It was a new year, but I was looking back–marveling at where my journey had started with Tunigo and where it had come to since. In just five years, I had witnessed firsthand and up close the evolution of a formidable music team and ascended to a leadership position in the music industry in a trajectory that felt nothing short of extraordinary. This moment was a testament to that growth and the realization that distant dreams had become my vision and reality.

A month later, I was part of a team at Spotify that earned the number-three spot on Billboard's 2019 Power 100 list in recognition of our work as "the dominant streaming service that had helped save the recorded-music business" and "whose stock sales have benefited labels and their artists." Along with Spotify founder and CEO Daniel Ek, Chief Content Officer Dawn Ostroff, Chief Financial Officer Barry McCarthy, and General Counsel and Vice President of Legal Affairs Horacio Gutierrez, I was recognized for innovation in an industry of creatives. It was a pinnacle moment, and it was almost surreal.

Despite all of these successes and milestones, I was the guy who loved creating a Swedish start-up and who was now working for a global corporation with thousands of employees. I am an entrepreneur at heart and after seven years at Spotify, I no longer felt like much of one.

After a fulfilling seven-year tenure at Spotify, where I had achieved more than I ever imagined, I observed a shift in dynamics. The company had grown from an underdog to an industry leader, but in the process, some of the entrepreneurial zeal that had driven me faded. This feeling was further amplified by our move to the large office complex at 4 World Trade and the organizational changes that followed.

I realized that it was time for me to move on.

I left as the Global Head of Music in September 2019 but remained a Senior Advisor for another six months. During the period when I was still an advisor, I wanted to explore a concept I had been contemplating – linking today´s streaming companies with Times Square, reminiscent of the MTV "Total Request Live" era.

From the NFL and Cirque de Soleil to TSX Entertainment

If you are a regular in Times Square, you may have observed that there are a lot of old buildings owned by the same owners for years. I wasn't seeing a lot of potential opportunity to break in (and let's not even talk about rent prices). However, in 2019, a newer building at 20 Times Square had an opening after an interesting collab between the NFL and Cirque de Soleil failed to gain traction.

In the bustling winter of 2018, amid a whirlwind of travel and a packed schedule, my assistant relayed that Phil Meynell had been trying to contact me regarding a potential opportunity with Spotify at a venue in Times Square. Phil was consulting for Maefield Developments, the landlord of 20 Times Square, who was searching for a new tenant. While these discussions did not culminate in a partnership, they opened the door to a valuable connection with Fortress Investment Group, the financial backbone of the property, less than two years later.

Likewise, this professional interaction with Phil Meynell evolved into a personal friendship. Two years following our initial meeting, Phil would become an integral part of TSX Entertainment, taking on the role of Vice President of Creative and Entertainment. This turn of events underscores how unpredictable and fruitful networking in the business world can be and that potential opportunities can transform into lasting relationships.

An agreement for the property at 20 Times Square, under the management of Maefield Development, proved elusive. In the backdrop, Fortress Investment Group, an investment manager with $50 billion under management and a wealth of experience in the entertainment sector, was paying close attention. Their interest was piqued by the prospect of an entertainment-led real estate strategy instead of a traditional retail-driven experience.

During our discussions regarding 20 Times Square, I could sense the palpable interest from Dean Dakolias, Managing Partner and Co-Chief Investor, Pete Briger, the founder and principal, and Ivan Yee, Managing Director at Fortress. They were captivated by the vision I laid out for 20 Times Square.

"What you are looking for on steroids."

During these conversations, they broached the subject of TSX Broadway, a project just across the street. They saw it as a match for my ambitions but with even greater potential. "This," they suggested, "offers the flexibility you are seeking, but amplified—what you are looking for on steroids."

This project was originally intended to be a large-scale retail venture. However, the rise of e-commerce and the subsequent decline of flagship stores forced a rethink in strategy. This was where my vision came into play, offering a fresh direction for the building and the times.

My vision was inspired by the unique positioning of the TSX building, situated at the busiest intersection in the Western Hemisphere.

This iconic location, visited by over 100 million people annually, was chosen with a singular aim: to captivate and entertain. Times Square, historically the heart of entertainment, brimmed with attractions like MTV's "TRL," the colossal Virgin Megastore, and the immersive Toys "R" Us flagship store. Yet, as the landscape evolved, the area became dominated by fast food joints and souvenir shops, diluting its original allure.

In response to this shift, my strategy focused on reclaiming Times Square's entertainment legacy. By introducing the first-ever permanent stage in Times Square, we envisioned spectacular events that would capture the attention of visitors, residents, and fans. This stage would serve as the cornerstone for generating buzz and drawing crowds into the building, where they would discover a plethora of entertainment offerings, pop-up retail spaces, and integrated hospitality experiences.

The concept extends beyond mere entertainment; it is more about allowing artists and brands to temporarily "own" parts or even the entirety of the building. This approach fosters a truly dynamic environment where experiences are continually refreshed, ensuring relevance in the fast-paced world of pop culture. The building itself is envisaged as a creative playground, offering boundless possibilities for innovation and engagement.

This vision aimed to revive Times Square's entertainment heritage but also to set a new standard for interactive and immersive experiences in one of the world's most vibrant locales.

Following our initial discussions, I found myself at Fortress HQ, sitting across from Dean and Ivan. I made my stance clear: I was not after a consultant role. Instead, half-joking yet with a serious undertone, I proposed a bold idea: "If you are genuinely invested in the entertainment vision and are considering building a new Top 10 entertainment company centered around that building, then that's something I would be interested in."

Their response was measured, reflecting the enormity of their investment. "We're navigating almost $3 billion in this project," Dean explained, their caution evident. "Diving all in on one concept is daunting, so we have to keep our options open." They promised to reconvene with a decision in a couple of weeks.

Two weeks later…their decision was firm and exciting: "We are ready to take the next step," Dean and Ivan announced. "Let's establish a joint venture to take this business plan further." We agreed that the vision was to secure a lease for the first 10 floors of the TSX Building if this step was successful.

This proposition was exactly the catalyst we needed, setting the stage for a venture that could redefine the entertainment landscape. This joint venture would not only embody our shared vision but also mark a significant transformation in the heart of one of the world's most vibrant locations.

We started to really talk. And we talked some more. The conversation continued until we signed a deal in March 2020– two weeks *after* New York had essentially closed down due to the pandemic.

On one hand, the timing was terrible. Yet, on the flip side, it presented a unique chance to share my vision. With everyone confined at home, uncertain of what lay ahead, they were very receptive to listening.

The responses I received from artists, managers, and industry insiders were astonishingly positive. The vision was bold, perhaps even bordering on audacious, requiring a mix of fortune, perfect timing, and significant financial backing.

Fan-Powered Futures | 69

Whenever I posed the question, "Is this too far-fetched, or is it feasible?" the enthusiasm in their replies was palpable.

"I love it, and I believe in it," they'd say, followed invariably by, "How can I be a part of this? Is there a chance to invest?"

We decided to initiate a limited equity round, extending invitations to select individuals to join. The response was overwhelming, and virtually everyone we approached chose to invest. This included luminaries like The Weeknd and his manager Sal, Austin Rosen from Electric Feel (manager of Post Malone), and Chris Zarou from Visionary Group, among other eminent figures from the industry.

Their unanimous commitment was a powerful indicator that we were on the brink of something truly monumental.

Disneyland meets Las Vegas in the Big Apple

I envisioned a playground for artists and brands in the epicenter of entertainment–Times Square, which welcomes more than 400,000 visitors every single day. It would be a place where artists could perform, meet fans, sell merch, and create memorable experiences. I often described it as "Disneyland meets Las Vegas" with a digital underlying platform to take the experience globally.

The vision for TSX Entertainment was audacious: to establish the premier beacon in pop culture. Our goal transcended music; it encompassed the myriad verticals that shape pop culture, including fashion, television/movies, gaming, and sports.

It was becoming increasingly evident that the boundaries among these verticals were blurring. Artists were venturing beyond their original domains, eager to extend their brands into new realms of pop culture.

Similarly, influential pop culture brands were looking for new and broader partnerships. Our ambition was to position TSX as the paramount hub for bridging the gap between brands and fans, situating it in the most bustling locale in the Western Hemisphere.

Clearly, this ambition was big and broad, but with the right team and the right direction, I knew we could turn this gem of an idea into a bold dream come true.

CHAPTER 6

The Paradigm Shift to Fan Engagement

With TSX Entertainment, I finally found a project that resonated deeply with my vision for the future of entertainment and hospitality.

This alignment felt like a prelude to playing a significant role in an emerging industry shift. A critical aspect of this vision was rethinking the traditional concept of "consumers," especially within the vibrant realm of pop culture.

The goal of today's brand strategy, particularly in pop culture, is to transform customers who passively buy products into raving fans who follow a brand or artist's every move. But achieving this requires a profound understanding of the evolution of fandom. Where did it all begin?

The broadcast era casts a wide net

Reflecting on the history of brand and customer interactions, it always comes back to the broadcast model.

About 15 years ago, the relationship between brands and customers was largely unidirectional. Major brands would deploy extensive TV commercials, print ads, and outdoor advertising to persuade consumers who viewed the ads to purchase their products.

This communication strategy focused primarily on showcasing a product's price or quality, aiming to appeal to as broad an audience as possible. However, options for reaching the masses were limited due to the high costs associated with these traditional channels. It was a start, but it was definitely not about fandom at this point.

The only place where you see this model succeed regularly today is the Super Bowl. While the ads cost a fortune, they also reach across state lines, demographics, and interests as more and more people report greater interest in the commercials than in the big game itself and spend days talking about their favorites.

Creating fandom in the digital age

The advent of the digital revolution finally leveled the playing field, drastically altering the landscape of consumer engagement. The era of communal TV watching, where shows acted as cultural campfires, gave way to a fragmented media consumption model.

American households, which had previously averaged nearly nine hours of TV watching each day as the calendar flipped to the year 2000, saw this number drop to an average of just three hours by 2023[1]. At the same time, online engagement surged, with the average American spending approximately seven hours per day on the internet in 2023[2].

This transition from a broadcast to an engagement model marked the end of easy mass reach through TV commercials

---

[1] Cramer-Flood, Ethan. "US Time Spent with Media 2022." Insider Intelligence. Accessed Feb. 5, 2024. https://www.insiderintelligence.com/content/us-time-spent-with-media-2022
[2] Moody, Rebecca. "Screen Time Statistics: Average Screen Time in the US Vs. the Rest of the World." Comparitech. Accessed Feb. 5, 2024. https://www.comparitech.com/tv-streaming/screen-time-statistics/

tied to popular shows. Instead, the focus shifted towards a direct-to-consumer (DTC) approach, necessitating innovative strategies to connect with and engage consumers.

The challenge was no longer about reaching an audience but cultivating a community of fans.

A new audience and a new approach

The transformation in how people consume media and interact with brands demanded a new approach. The question became: How do we engage meaningfully with consumers in a landscape saturated with digital content? The objective was clear: to turn passive consumers into active fans, creating a symbiotic relationship where engagement and loyalty run deep.

While exploring the strategies and philosophies underpinning this shift towards fan engagement and delving into the importance of creating experiences that resonate on a truly personal level, I believe it is all about fostering a sense of belonging and community among fans.

There is a reason people spend an inordinate amount of money to see a concert and buy the merch. Live entertainment makes us feel something. You just can't get the emotional pull of emotions and a shared cultural moment with friends through a digital-only experience.

Through the lens of TSX, we could more clearly see the potential of spaces and platforms that could facilitate these connections, redefining the future of entertainment and hospitality along the way.

New paradigms of "consumer" and new metrics for success: Experiences over goods

Today's metrics for success have evolved significantly from the broadcast era's focus on quality and price. The dynamics are now all about *convenience*, *access*, and *exclusivity*. This change reflects a deeper transformation in consumer values, with a pronounced preference for *experiences* over mere possession of *goods*.

However, the most forward-thinking companies have discovered a way to blend these elements, harnessing immersive experiences to enhance product launches and purchases.

Quality and price are still important, but they are no longer the sole determinants of consumer interest. Convenience and access are paramount in the digital age.

Consumers value the ease with which they can obtain products and services as well as the exclusivity offered. This exclusivity is not just about the scarcity of products; it's more about the unique experiences brands can provide.

Brands that recognize and capitalize on this shift have seen remarkable success, creating memorable moments that resonate deeply with their audience. "Barbenheimer," the epic convergence of the release of summer blockbuster movies "Barbie" and "Oppenheimer" in the summer of 2023, created a cultural moment that lingered long past the release. Fans rushed to see the double-header, returned again, and cheered the films on to many wins across film award categories.

Taylor Swift's epic "The Eras Tour" tapped into another incredible cultural moment. Most people agree she was "the" most talked about person in 2023, and her concert, complete with friendship bracelets and fans of literally all ages, had a big part to do with her being named "TIME" magazine's person of the year (not to mention the economic impact she had on each city she visited).

A season of touchdowns

In illustrating the transformative power of fans, the romance between Taylor Swift and Kansas City Chiefs star tight end Travis Kelce stands as a compelling case study. Swift's presence at Chiefs' games following her relationship with Kelce did more than just bridge the worlds of pop music and football; it catalyzed a significant shift in viewership dynamics.

Suddenly, a wave of young girls, previously indifferent to or uninterested in football, found themselves eagerly tuning into NFL games in hopes of catching a glimpse of their favorite pop star and her entourage. This phenomenon went beyond mere celebrity intrigue to become a testament to how fan engagement can transcend traditional boundaries and foster new communities of enthusiasts. This same group cheered wildly as the Chiefs won the Super Bowl in early 2024, not letting their interest flag for a single moment.

The impact of this newfound interest was quantifiable and substantial.

Apex Marketing reported that Swift's association with the Chiefs and her attendance at NFL games effectively generated an additional $331.5 million in brand value for the team and the league. This staggering figure underscores not merely the economic implications but the profound influence of fan bases in shaping perceptions and enhancing the value of sports franchises.

Yet, the "Taylor Swift effect" extends beyond the immediate financial boon to the NFL. It highlights the broader power of fans in today's cultural and entertainment landscapes. Fans are no longer passive recipients of content; they are active participants, capable of driving significant attention and reshaping narratives. Their engagement is key to unlocking new demographics and expanding the reach of brands, artists, and sports leagues.

This example encapsulates the essence of the new fan paradigm—a shift towards recognizing and leveraging the dynamic role of fans in propelling success and fostering expansive, inclusive communities around shared interests. The synergistic relationship between Taylor Swift, Travis Kelce, and the NFL vividly illustrates the potential of embracing and nurturing fan engagement.

A shifting reality

The advent of immersive technologies has opened up new avenues for combining experiences with goods.

Virtual and augmented reality, for example, allow brands to offer unique, immersive experiences that complement their products. This blend of physical and digital experiences enhances the consumer's interaction with the product and creates a more profound connection with the brand. We will focus on this more later, but it is interesting to see how technology is impacting fandom.

Coca-Cola, for instance, did a bang-up job of using social media, augmented reality, and an age-old product to garner headlines in 2022. They launched "Coca-Cola Creations," mysterious new soda flavors designed to spark conversation.

Coke started with the release of "Starlight," a flavor intended to be "space-flavored," and added an augmented-reality concert from Ava Max that required a QR code from a can of Starlight to watch. Sugar Byte, which supposedly tasted like pixels, came next–and the company launched it in the "Fortnite" video game. Two months later, Coca-Cola took over Twitch and invited Marshmello to the party.

You get the point: A relatively low-budget campaign was so creative that people kept talking about Coke and trying to get their hands on these limited-release flavors *all year long*.

The most successful companies today are those that have managed to integrate experiences into their product launches in an effective and interesting way. These brands understand that an event or an experience can elevate a product from being a mere item to becoming a cultural phenomenon.

An Apple a day and hitting the Target bullseye

Think about Apple's product launches. They are never about just unveiling a new device. These newsworthy events are more about creating an experience that captivates a global audience.

Apple excels at creating and keeping loyal customers and fans. Yes, they put out traditional press releases and email alerts, but they go much further to create a sense of hype and anticipation.

Apple uses storytelling to create must-see hints at what is to come. They leak strategic information about the upcoming product. They offer exclusive previews to a selected group of influencers and innovators. They use a simple but powerful design for every product so that merely the experience of opening the box is magical. They make headlines on launch day and for weeks to come. Apple also offers personalized settings and preferences that make their fans feel truly recognized and understood.

It all started when Apple launched the Macintosh computer during the Super Bowl in 1984 with a commercial directed by filmmaker Ridley Scott. Their groundbreaking product launches have continued with the iPod, iPad, Apple Watch, and the Apple Vision Pro. Apple doesn't just create consumers–it sparks repeat business with its wide and rapid fan base.

Similarly, pop-up shops and exclusive events have become a staple for fashion and lifestyle brands, offering a unique blend of exclusivity and engagement. The Target website crashed when the company launched its bargain Missoni for Target line, and its partnership with designer Lilly Pulitzer also sold out in a frenzy in just hours. All of a sudden, this big-box retailer developed a reputation for affordable high-end fashion, which was a must-have.

The ultimate goal for any brand in today's market is to create a cohesive experience surrounding their product. This approach not only drives engagement and loyalty but also sets the brand apart in a crowded marketplace.

By focusing on convenience, access, and exclusivity and by prioritizing immersive experiences, brands can connect with their audiences on a deeper level, turning customers into advocates and fans.

The dual purpose of products in the digital age

In today's consumer culture, products serve a dual purpose that transcends their practical utility. A pair of new sneakers or a luxury handbag does more than facilitate mobility or carry essentials; these items act as extensions of your personality, playing a crucial role in self-expression and identity formation.

Social media platforms amplify personal messages and express values, giving individuals the chance to declare, "This is who I am" or "This is who I aspire to be." This dual communication—conveying utility and identity—is a cornerstone of engagement for new generations.

What you wear, listen to, and consume speaks volumes about your personality, dreams, and identity. This isn't an entirely new phenomenon–consumption has always been a mode of self-expression. However, the scale and visibility provided by social media have greatly amplified its importance.

Every choice, from the brands we support to the products we flaunt, serves as a deliberate statement of our values, preferences, and aspirations, instantly broadcasted to a global audience.

Individuals can now curate and share their lives on a variety of platforms to highlight their choices and affiliations.

This digital showcase is not just about vanity; it is a form of communication that tells a story of who we are and what we stand for. It's also a way to connect with like-minded individuals, find a community, and sometimes differentiate oneself in a crowded digital landscape.

The quest for attention in the digital age has led to what many refer to as the "attention economy." In this economy, the most valuable commodity is not money or goods but the attention of others.

Cutting through the noise to capture and retain this fan-based attention is a significant challenge for brands and artists, especially when everyone is vying for a moment in the spotlight. Brands and individuals alike strive to create content and messages that resonate, hoping to establish a connection in an increasingly fragmented media landscape.

In the attention economy, success often hinges on the ability to stand out to offer something genuinely engaging or unique.

For brands, this means creating products and experiences that serve practical purposes and carry symbolic weight, enabling consumers to express their identities and values.

For individuals, it means navigating a deluge of content to find and share what truly represents them. The challenge and opportunity exist in creating narratives and connections that resonate deeply enough to cut through all the noise and capture the precious currency of attention in a world where everyone is a broadcaster and attention spans are short.

The transformative power of fandom in modern culture

The concept of fandom has undergone a profound transformation in the music industry as well as in other global businesses and industries. This evolution is epitomized by the practice of naming fan bases, a strategy that not only fosters a sense of belonging and community but also turns fans into the most potent ambassadors for their favorite artists.

Fans definitely appreciate a closer connection with their favorite artists, and artists benefit from this, in turn.

Rihanna's Fenty Beauty brand netted more than $600 million in its first 15 months, and her Savage x Fenty lingerie brand–known for being both inclusive and affordable–is valued at more than $1 billion. She creatively streamed its launch via Amazon Prime runway shows.

Successful artists across genres have begun naming their fan bases, creating a unique identity that fans can rally around. Taylor Swift's "Swifties," BTS' "Army," and Justin Bieber's "Beliebers" are all prime examples of how this strategy cultivates a deep sense of unity and belonging among fans. Not everyone can achieve superstardom or fame, but everyone can participate in this success along the way.

Fans gain a broader global community and, in turn, their collective actions, from social media engagement to word-of-mouth promotion, further amplify the artist's reach and influence.

Today, the relationship between artists and fans is more critical and close than ever. Modern fans harbor expectations far beyond those of previous generations. They seek more personal interactions, such as selfies with their idols, and they closely follow their favorite artists' every move, ready at a moment's notice to share messages that resonate with them.

However, this relationship can be a double-edged sword: Fans who feel betrayed or let down by artists or brands they once supported quickly express their dissatisfaction, often publicly and vehemently. Arctic Monkeys fans turned on the band in droves when they got more popular and evolved into a more mainstream sound. Eminem's fans either tear him down for his past misogynistic and homophobic comments (which he has apologized for and said he regrets) or defend him for the same thing.

It can be hard to win and keep the same rabid fans for the long run. It can be hard to devise newer and more creative strategies that support personalization and fan engagement.

The phrase "Fans will hire you, but they will also fire you" encapsulates the delicate balance of the modern artist-fan relationship. Today's fans may give a lot, but they also expect a lot in return.

Fans' expectations for authenticity, engagement, and alignment with their values are higher than ever. When these expectations are met, fans can be incredibly loyal and supportive. However, any perceived deviation from these values can lead to swift backlash.

Artists and brands must navigate this complex landscape carefully, balancing the desire for broad appeal with the need to maintain the trust and respect of their core fan base.

CHAPTER 7

The Roots of Passion – A Brief History of Fandom

From the halls of ancient Rome echoing with the roar of chariot-racing fans to the fervent devotees of modern-day pop stars, the power of fandom has shaped culture and society for centuries. The word "fan" may be relatively new, but the phenomenon it describes—ardent devotion to a person, team, work of art, or cause—is as old as humanity. The history of fandom is rich and has had a transformative influence on how we experience and interact with the world.

The early days: before "fan"

While the term "fan" didn't emerge until the late 19th century, when it became an abbreviated form of "fanatic," passionate communities have long existed around beloved figures, activities, and ideas. Gladiators of ancient Rome commanded legions of devoted supporters, their victories and defeats fueling heated debates and fanatical loyalty. Religious devotees throughout history have exemplified intense connection with their chosen figures of worship, shaping communities and inspiring works of art.

The rise of literary culture in the 17th and 18th centuries gave birth to new forms of fandom. Authors like William Shakespeare and Jane Austen amassed passionate followings, with readers engaging in discussions, analysis, and even the creation of their own derivative works. These early forms of transformative fandom foreshadowed the creative power fans would wield in centuries to come.

The birth of modern fandom: Sherlock and the revolution

The late 19th and early 20th centuries saw the explosion of popular culture and the emergence of modern fandom. Perhaps no figure exemplifies this shift more than the fictional detective Sherlock Holmes. Sir Arthur Conan Doyle's compelling detective stories captured the public imagination, spawning a fervent fandom unlike anything seen before. His readers did more than just consume the stories – they *engaged* with them.

Sherlockian fans mourned the detective's "death" in "The Final Problem," wearing black armbands and pressuring Doyle to resurrect his beloved character. This marked a turning point in the world of fandom: Fans were no longer just passive recipients but became active participants in the worlds they loved. They also began to create their own stories, artwork, and communities centered around Sherlock Holmes, establishing the foundation of modern fan culture.

Pulp fandom: sci-fi takes the stage

The 1920s and '30s witnessed the rise of pulp magazines, a breeding ground for science fiction, fantasy, and horror. It was here that organized fandom truly took root. Enthusiasts formed clubs, published fanzines, and hosted conventions – creating a participatory culture around their shared interests. Science fiction fandom, in particular, developed a unique jargon ("fanspeak"), a tradition of pseudonymous writing, and a culture of collaboration and critique.

This period also saw the emergence of "media fandom," where devotion centered on films and television shows rather than purely literary sources. With their passionate embrace of Star Trek, Trekkies became emblematic of this phenomenon. You might be surprised to learn that the original show only aired for three seasons. However, its cult following kept the love alive for decades to come.

We can also see the early seeds of young fandom in The Mickey Mouse Club, which debuted in 1955 and cemented that generation's lifelong passion for all things Disney. Its young fans fell in love with Annette Funicello, helping her garner a record deal, and proudly wore Mouseketeer ears and other merch as a representation of their devotion.

These early fans laid the groundwork for the vibrant online fandoms of today.

The explosion of fan culture

The second half of the 20th century witnessed a dramatic expansion and diversification of fandom. Japanese manga and anime found a global audience, giving rise to their own passionate fan communities. The advent of home video allowed fans to rewatch and analyze beloved movies and shows at will, fostering deeper engagement. And as cultural phenomena like *Star Wars* and *Harry Potter* captured the world's attention, fandom became firmly entrenched in mainstream culture.

Two significant forces shaped fandom in this period:

1. **Female-Led Fandoms:** Women, often sidelined in earlier fan communities, began to drive fan culture. Slash

fiction, which explored romantic relationships between fictional characters (often same-sex), was pioneered primarily by female fans, challenging traditional narratives and empowering creative expression.

2. **Technology as a Catalyst:** Bulletin boards and early online forums provided a space for fans to connect regardless of location, fostering communities that could not have existed offline. This prefigured the transformative power the internet would later have on fandom.

The internet age: fandom unleashed

The internet revolutionized fandom, providing unprecedented opportunities for connection, creation, and collective action. No longer limited by geography or access to niche publications, fans found their tribes online. From sprawling fan fiction archives to vibrant Tumblr communities, the internet fostered an explosion of fan creativity and collaboration.

Social media platforms further amplified fan voices. Fans could interact directly with creators, organize campaigns, and mobilize globally for causes related to their fandoms. No longer just consumers, fans became powerful stakeholders in the cultural landscape, thanks to the internet's global reach.

This period also saw increased intersectionality within fandom. Marginalized groups found space to explore their identities through shared passions, challenging dominant narratives within popular culture. Fans are now free to use their platforms to address issues like representation, diversity, and social justice within their beloved fandoms and beyond.

Fandom in the 21st century: A force to be reckoned with

Today, fandom is a ubiquitous and influential force, shaping the entertainment industry, driving social change, and redefining the relationship between creators and audiences. Key trends in contemporary fandom include:

1. **Global Reach:** Fandom is now a truly global phenomenon, transcending borders and cultures. The rise of K-pop and international cinema has brought together fans worldwide, creating dynamic cross-cultural exchanges. Fans extend across time zones, languages, and locations to connect over the people, places, and things they love.

2. **Transmedia Experiences:** Fans don't just consume one form of media. Today, they immerse themselves in interconnected worlds spanning movies, games, comics, and beyond, fueling a desire for rich and expansive narratives.

3. **Fan-Creator Symbiosis:** The line between fan and creator has continued to blur. Fan works often garner tremendous attention, with some even transitioning into "official" canon. Creators actively engage with fans, recognizing their influence and incorporating feedback into their work.

4. **Activist Fandom:** Fans mobilize around social and political issues spurred by their passions. From charity drives to campaigns for representation, fandoms harness their collective power for meaningful change.

Fans can no longer be dismissed or sidelined–they are clearly a force to be reckoned with.

The rise of fandom, however, has not been without challenges. Issues like toxicity within online communities, online harassment, and the blurring of boundaries between fans and creators underscore the need for responsible participation and ethical fan practices. The struggle for inclusivity and equitable representation within fandoms also remains an ongoing concern.

The future of fandom

Fandom, once a subculture, is now mainstream.

It is a testament to the enduring power of passion, community, and creativity. As technology continues to evolve, so, too, will fandom. Virtual and augmented reality have the potential to revolutionize fan experiences. Increased emphasis on diversity and inclusion is crucial for the continued growth and positive impact of fandom.

Fandom isn't merely about what we love, but about who we are and the world we desire to build. By understanding the history of fandom, we gain valuable insights into the transformative power of shared passion and its potential to shape the future.

CHAPTER 8

From Disney to TSX: Crafting a Legacy of Fandom

In the evolving landscape of entertainment and business, TSX Entertainment was created for this moment of fandom–to take advantage of the monumental shift in how brands engage and connect with audiences. This relationship wields unparalleled influence and momentum and can transcend traditional boundaries of engagement and loyalty.

The term "'brand" assumes a multifaceted role, often interchanged with artists, innovators, creators, and influencers. This intentional lexicon shift reflects a broader truth: We inhabit a world increasingly dominated by the essence and ethos of brands.

This paradigm goes beyond the concept of visibility or market presence to encompass cultivating a shared set of values and a sense of belonging that deeply resonates with individuals.

Today, we see brands that have successfully broadened their horizons, venturing into uncharted territories far beyond their original domains. 3M was founded more than a century ago as a mining company. Today, many people think of Post-It Notes when 3M comes to mind, but the company now spans medical supplies, worker safety, graphics, transportation, and much more.

Netflix was originally just DVDs that you could rent via mail, which evolved into a subscription model and then into streaming–ultimately making its original business model obsolete. Now, Netflix is well-known for its award-winning original series and movies. And don't forget Amazon–you might not even recall that the multidimensional global behemoth was once simply an online bookstore.

These narratives are testaments to the power of brand loyalty, the strategic infusion of core values into brand identity, and the trust meticulously built with fans over time. Transitioning from mere endorsements to collaborations signifies a monumental shift in strategy.

Today, artists and brands alike are eager to diversify their appeal, reaching out to new audiences through innovative products and immersive experiences.

How K-pop turned a pandemic low point into a must-see moment

K-pop (short for Korean popular music) stands as a beacon of excellence in fan engagement when it comes to music. It deftly demonstrates how to cultivate profoundly strong relationships with fans. K-pop offers many amazing beyond-the-music experiences, ranging from concerts and merchandise to unique, fan-centric products and moments.

During the pandemic lockdown, when everyone was sheltering at home, the wildly popular BTS sold a record-breaking 993,000 tickets for their virtual weekend concert, with fans tuning in from *191 different countries.* The event was originally planned as a live concert, but the band quickly pivoted to an interactive, immersive experience where fans were still visible on the screens during the show and had the opportunity to pick one of six cameras as their viewpoint.

Bank Si-hyuk, the founder and CEO of Hybe/Big Hit Music, the label behind BTS, cited Disney and Apple as examples of brands that inspired the creation of the label and the band BTS.

Disney's blueprint for building enduring relationships through storytelling and diverse experiences—from amusement parks and hotels to movies, TV shows, and merchandise—set the gold standard in creating deeply impactful connections with fans.

The Disney magic inspires TSX Entertainment

Reflecting on the frenzy surrounding Disney's blockbuster "Frozen," where the quest for Elsa costumes and other merch became a near-herculean task for parents worldwide, it is easy to see the magnitude of the influence that particular brands can wield. Stories of parents going to extraordinary lengths, such as fighting to purchase an Elsa doll for $1,200 on eBay, underscore the emotional investment and loyalty fans are willing to commit to their beloved brands.

The seeds of today's fan-centric strategies were sewn long ago.

Disney's model of expanding into various verticals based on sustained fan relationships was a significant source of inspiration for TSX Entertainment. For us, it is more than just emulation; it is about understanding and innovating on the principles of fan engagement and brand expansion.

As we created TSX, we focused keenly on developing the right guiding philosophy, a unique compass to direct our collective vision. We started by formulating a set of core beliefs with our leadership team, serving as the bedrock for product development and experience creation.

In addition to the critical importance of access, convenience, and exclusivity, these core beliefs for TSX include the need to delight customers with contextual, frictionless interactions, a focus on seamless end-to-end journeys that are driven through an app, and the recognition that real growth comes through community development and empowerment.

These principles not only provide a reference point for the entire TSX organization to align with and critically assess over time but also underscore the necessity of adaptability for sustained success. Our ultimate aim is defined by a broad, overarching objective that acts as our north star.

Inspired by Spotify's approach, we tailored a similar framework to suit our unique context. At TSX, we champion beliefs such as the significance of access, convenience, and exclusivity in enhancing fan experiences, the pivotal role of cultural currency within the creator ecosystem, and the symbiotic relationship between in-person and digital interactions, amplifying their collective impact. All of these convictions inform both our strategic and immediate goals, offering clear direction to our team.

Additionally, we adhere to certain "truths" that further shape our strategy.

For instance, recognizing that "Creators run the show" highlights the industry's evolution toward direct artist-fan connections. "Fans craving more" acknowledges the digital era's double-edged sword—the ample ease of discovery alongside some significant challenges in artist-fan engagement. Moreover, understanding that "Creators have become brands" reflects the modern artist's expanded influence beyond traditional boundaries.

Front and center in Times Square

With these foundations, TSX is poised to revolutionize entertainment and empower even more innovative artists and brands to deliver unparalleled immersive experiences.

A prime illustration of this vision was the launch of the TSX Billboard, an expansive 18,000-square-foot billboard in Times Square. Eschewing conventional advertising models, we fostered a more engaging, participatory experience for fans, pioneering the integration of an app for interactive content display and direct audio streaming, reimagining outdoor media through technology.

Our ambition for the TSX billboard—envisioned as "The world's largest social feed"—was to transcend traditional advertising by enabling individual content creation and expression, bridging the digital and physical realms. The debut of PixelStar, just ahead of New Year's Eve as the calendar flipped from 2022 to 2023, exemplifies this. As the first feature on the TSX app, PixelStar allows users to commandeer a prominent Times Square billboard via their smartphones for personal celebrations and expressions, mirroring social media engagement but on a much more monumental scale.

Since its inception, PixelStar has seen exponential growth, introducing innovative features such as sound to enable a dynamic platform where fans and artists interact on equal footing.

As the TSX billboard became a pivotal cultural hub in Times Square, drawing crowds for everything from Super Bowl viewings to movie premieres and big video game releases, our visibility surged. However, with our space still under construction and an estimated 18 months until its completion, not to mention the looming threat of a recession, we encountered a fresh set of challenges.

The initial months of 2023 presented one unprecedented roadblock after another.

The lingering effects of the pandemic had already hampered our expansion efforts, and the situation was further exacerbated by soaring interest rates, which reached unparalleled highs. Add in a generally adverse macroeconomic climate globally, and suddenly securing new capital and investments was a truly formidable task. The urgency to demonstrate the viability of our business model and captivate potential stakeholders grew increasingly acute.

The economic turmoil was not unique to TSX; it cast a shadow over the entire business landscape. Many companies, especially startups, found themselves in dire straits, and a significant number of them were forced to shutter their operations amid the harsh conditions.

To navigate through these turbulent times, we clearly needed to execute a groundbreaking strategy that would draw fresh interest and chart a renewed course towards success.

Who knew that Post Malone would be a big part of it? Honestly, I might have guessed.

CHAPTER 9

Post Malone: This is the coolest venue in the f**ing universe

Picture this: A countdown clock slowly ticks down as passersby, police, and swarms of people gather in Times Square. A few harried New Yorkers hurry by, but most pause and look, realizing that something big is in the works.

Hints of something to come have been dropped on social media, and the crowd is abuzz with wonder: What was going to happen? Who was going to appear? What was the countdown for?

Then, at 5:30 p.m. on July 18, 2023, out walks Post Malone onto the TSX stage in the heart of Times Square, *literally* stopping traffic as he launched into his new single "Overdrive."

Post was the first-ever performer to take the stage, which sits behind the now-famous 18,000-square-foot billboard, and we could not have asked for a better partner in this crazy venture– a crazy venture that almost didn't happen.

He told the crowd, "I'm so grateful and so very honored to be kicking this off. This is the coolest venue in the f-ing universe."

I couldn't agree more…

Now picture this: Just three hours earlier, we had suddenly lost the permit for the show due to safety concerns, and it was raining–and not a light summer mist. It was pouring, although the forecast gave us some small glimmer of hope.

I had never felt so alone and so worried.

The concert and Clios that almost didn't happen

This surprise concert with Post was the first of its kind, and it was a huge risk. It was also no small effort.

We had secured a permit for a 15-minute concert in Times Square that was pulled at the last minute, only to be restored, thanks to some friends in high places who I will forever be grateful to. We had been juggling logistics from long-lens cameras to press passes, security, budgets, and more for weeks. It was a test of the TSX, Times Square, and the power of fans.

We had asked Post Malone to be our debut artist on the stage because he is pretty much perfect. He is professional, polite, on time, and generally amazing.

When he agreed, "I'll do it," I knew New York was in for an incredible treat. We secretly flew him in on a private jet so he could entertain the Times Square crowd in between his busy concert schedule.

The backstory of the artist fated to be a legend

When his "Beerbongs & Bentleys" album was released in 2018, Post Malone was on the cusp of stardom, recognized within the industry but not yet the household name he was destined to become. The new album presented an opportunity not just for Post Malone but also for the curatorial acumen of Spotify's editorial team.

Interestingly, the song "Rockstar" emerged as a contentious point in internal discussions regarding the album's lead single.

While the Spotify team was convinced of its massive potential, not everyone believed it should be the first single. Nevertheless, guided by our insights and unique positioning within the music ecosystem, the Spotify team championed "Rockstar" as the album's leading track, securing its placement on New Music Friday and integrating it into major playlists, including Today's Top Hits—a decision that was not mirrored by other streaming services with the same conviction.

Our advocacy for "Rockstar" was more than a gamble: It was also a testament to our analytical prowess and understanding of the music landscape. The track not only catapulted to the top of the Billboard Hot 100, marking Post Malone's first number-one hit but also reinforced the significance of trust and vision in the music industry.

This success laid the foundation for a lasting relationship with Post Malone's management team–Austin Rosen, Bobby Greenleaf, and Dre London–built on a shared history of support and belief in Post's talent.

When the idea of the TSX Stage was still in its infancy, this relationship helped pave the way for what would become a defining moment in pop culture and fandom. Even though the stage had not yet been completed, Post's management was immediately enthusiastic about the potential.

The mutual respect and trust cultivated over time made the decision seamless, with Post Malone himself giving the nod to proceed.

This collaboration with Post Malone and his team had a little to do with launching a big, bold new stage, but it had a lot to do with making a statement in the pop culture landscape, showcasing the power of innovation, and the impact of nurturing relationships within the music industry.

Back to the future

With the permit again in place and the rain finally stopped, Post Malone showed 30,000 people why he will forever be one of my favorite artists.

The problem?

They wanted more, of course.

Our permit was for 15 minutes and 15 minutes only, and the crowd was egging him on for an encore. When he started to play again, my phone was literally on fire, and people were telling me I needed to pull him off the stage immediately. I knew that wasn't going to happen so I shut my phone off and enjoyed his last three minutes while my mind went into overdrive.

While I knew I was likely in a lot of hot water, it was hard not to marvel at this moment. Post Malone told the cheering crowd, "I'm the first guy to do this, and I was super terrified because I know everyone has a busy day and a busy schedule." At the conclusion of each song, he paused and made a heart shape with his hands to share some of the love back to both old and new fans.

The crowd went wild beyond my wildest dreams.

While he doesn't have a lot of product collaborations or endorsements, Post Malone is beloved by his fans because of his amazing sound and ability to connect with audiences and turn listeners into fans in a heartbeat.

And speaking of heartbeats, mine was beating pretty fast at the moment…

A one-time get-out-of-jail-free card

I knew we had broken the rules by going a few minutes over our 15-minute concert permit.

I knew we had screwed up, and I knew that safety was a paramount concern throughout the city at the time.

I also knew that New York needed us, and we needed New York.

Fortunately, all the positive comments from stakeholders, the media, and regular New Yorkers saved us. Ultimately, we did not break the rules on purpose and the concert was a smashing success for the city, Post Malone, and TSX Entertainment. We also agreed on new strictures going forward, recognizing that we were all in this for the long haul.

It took me a week to recover from that initial event. I told my wife I felt like I had just gone through open-heart surgery. I regularly got the chills, felt incredibly nauseous, and seemed to have a short-term case of PTSD, but eventually, the positivity and the event's overall good vibes won out.

Changing entertainment and Times Square forever

Post Malone's performance on the TSX Stage was a watershed event, a testament to the shared journey from his early days of emerging talent to becoming a global superstar.

It was a celebration of trust, timing, and the unyielding belief in the transformative power of music, marking the beginning of an era for the TSX Stage and setting a precedent for what was possible when visionaries come together to create unforgettable moments in pop culture.

What once seemed impossible was ultimately one of the most extraordinary events I have ever witnessed, and we continue to add more concerts, more events, and more headlines in this one-of-a-kind space.

The ultimate vindication and celebration came in the form of six Clio Awards for the Post Malone Times Square Takeover concert that we received with Republic Records. The Clios celebrates creativity across the entertainment world, honoring an industry that pushes boundaries and pervades pop culture, and these awards were truly the icing on the cake.

Part of fandom is disrupting norms, trying new and audacious things, and pushing boundaries. Thanks to Post Malone and a lot of great investors, politicians, and planners, we did just that.

CHAPTER 10

The Global Stage Awakens

The aftermath of the Post Malone spectacle at TSX was nothing short of miraculous. What once teetered on the brink of closure was now the epicenter of the entertainment industry's buzz.

Skeptics became believers overnight, their congratulations flooding in as emails and calls. Our inbox was a testament to this seismic shift, brimming with inquiries from artist managements, labels, big brands, and agencies, all echoing a singular desire: We want to be part of the TSX phenomenon.

The strategy behind TSX, particularly its stage, hinged on creating an aura of scarcity, a move that now proved prescient. The success of one event had sparked widespread interest, but the anticipation of what was next could solidify TSX as a cultural landmark.

Our ambition was unyielding: to establish the number-one tentpole in pop culture, a goal that now seemed within grasp.

As we sifted through the deluge of inquiries for our next venture, it was clear that diversification was key. The aim was to embrace genres beyond what had already been showcased, setting our sights on K-Pop and Latin music.

The challenge, however, lay in navigating the complexities of band availability. BTS and Blackpink, the titans of K-Pop, were momentarily out of reach, propelling us to search for alternatives.

Take two

The turning point came through an unexpected call from Steve Berman of Interscope Records, leading to a pivotal meeting with Hybe/Big Hit Entertainment, the label behind BTS.

The proposal was definitely intriguing: Jung Kook of BTS, a name synonymous with global fame, was poised to embark on a solo venture, an opportunity that aligned perfectly with our vision. Despite the hurdles faced post-Post Malone, we persuaded the city's administration to grant us the green light under strict guidelines.

Jung Kook's impending performance was not just another concert; it was a global spectacle. With live streaming, a merchandise garden in Times Square, and a meticulously planned promotion strategy, we set the stage for an unparalleled music event and experience.

Anticipation reached a fever pitch when Jung Kook hinted at a surprise for New York, sending the internet into a frenzy. He appeared on "The Today Show" the day before the surprise concert, further ratcheting up the excitement and interest level.

That night, fans started to line up outside our building.

We asked, "What are you waiting for?"

Their response? "We think Jung Kook is going to perform here tomorrow. We're not certain, but we are going to wait here all night because we would never forgive ourselves if we missed him!"

By the eve of the concert on November 9, 2023, the crowd had grown and grown and grown with wild speculation that had turned Times Square into a vigil of hope and excitement.

At 5 p.m., we announced that the one-and-only Jung Kook would be performing in 30 minutes. We shared Jung Kook content, played songs from his upcoming album, and created an instant karaoke party. At 5:25 p.m. the five-minute countdown timer started to tick.

When Jung Kook took the stage at 5:30, he was met with a roar that could rival the cacophony of Times Square on New Year's Eve. I thought our building might explode. The sound was so deafening.

The performance, which was streamed live to millions across the globe, was a testament to the unifying power of music, transcending geographical barriers and cultural divides.

The overall effect was staggering. The merch garden saw endless queues for the next five hours, a tangible marker of the event's impact. Jung showed immense appreciation for the BTS fans known as "The Army" in attendance, and it was amazing to see the connection between artist and fans.

The biggest problem was getting him out of there safely and efficiently. Eventually, the police suggested closing off traffic to 47th Street so that he could make a safe exit. Finally, Elvis had left the building.

More than an event, it was a cultural milestone

Beyond the immediate success, the analytics painted a broader picture of influence. Media monitor Critical Mention reported a total online audience of 4.8 billion, with earned media valued at $54 million. The event's reach was further underscored by the 10 million views on YouTube, highlighting the global resonance of TSX's endeavors.

Jung Kook's show at TSX was more than an event; it was a genuine cultural milestone that reinforced our position as a beacon in the landscape of global entertainment. The journey from near obscurity to hosting one of the most significant events in recent history was a testament to the power of vision, strategy, and the universal language of music. At its best, it was the trifecta of fandom, culture, and connection.

As we looked to the future, the possibilities seemed boundless.

We had succeeded not just in hosting an event, but in creating moments that transcended boundaries, connecting artists and fans in a shared experience of joy and unity. With the world as our stage, the journey ahead promised even greater heights, each step driven by the ambition to unite and inspire through the power of music. This, indeed, was just the beginning.

CHAPTER 11

The Third Time is a Charm for a New Times Square Dynasty

The neon-infused pulse of Times Square had never felt so alive. Two shows, two successes. The TSX Stage, my baby, had roared to life with raw, unadulterated star power – first with Post Malone's gritty swagger, then Jung Kook's electrifying K-Pop energy.

Now, it was time to make history. It was time to elevate this vision from a successful experiment to a bona fide pop-culture phenomenon.

"We need a woman," I'd asserted to the team, the decisiveness echoing in the stark white meeting room of TSX Entertainment. "A Latina legend, someone who has sold millions, has the hits, and will set this stage ablaze."

The response was unanimous – murmurs of approval and heads nodding vigorously. The seed was planted. We needed an icon.

Several names ricocheted across the table, but the room fell silent when the publicist, who also worked with Post Malone, dropped a bombshell: "Shakira is interested in performing at the TSX Stage."

The name hung in the air like a disco ball, shimmering with possibility. Shakira?

The room erupted in a cacophony of questions and barely contained excitement. I leaned back in my chair. Here was someone who checked every box... and more. A global superstar, a Latin icon, a legacy in the making. If we could land Shakira, this wouldn't just be a show but a coronation.

A match made in music heaven

Weeks of negotiations, logistics headaches, and late-night calls between New York and Miami ensued. Shakira was intrigued, and her label was hungry to leverage the buzz surrounding her upcoming album, "Las Mujeres Ya No Lloran." It was a perfect match – a superstar seeking to ignite a global comeback paired with a stage thirsting for its queen.

Word had leaked, of course. The internet was a rumbling volcano of speculation ever since Post Malone had hinted at more surprises coming to the TSX stage. Shakira's people, savvy as they were, played it coy and let the rumor mill churn.

The official announcement, crafted with the meticulous care of a diamond cutter, dropped with the precision of a Times Square confetti burst. "The New York Times" wanted to write a story about these big events in the middle of Times Square, complete with behind-the-scenes access – the promise of an exposé on how a spectacle of this magnitude was pulled together.

The day before the show, Shakira teased it on "The Tonight Show Starring Jimmy Fallon." Her playful smile radiated through the screen as she hinted at a New York surprise, her eyes sparkling with a mischievous glint. Social media went haywire, with millions of fans, not just hers, flooding Times Square.

Meanwhile, the tension was a palpable, living thing back at TSX Entertainment headquarters.

The Squared Division, renowned for their work with the biggest names in music, meticulously built out the stage. Their expertise, combined with Shakira's vision, promised a feast for the eyes as well as the ears, creating an LED video cube to showcase the star. The team buzzed with nervous energy. We had pulled off the impossible twice, and the pressure for a third miracle was immense.

We obtained permits to install speakers at Father Duffy Square and permission from the New York City Fire Department to use smoke as a special effect. While the NYPD had agreed that no one would be allowed to cross Seventh Avenue or Broadway between 45th and 47th streets, theatergoers were the exception. Every single detail was attended to with meticulous care and attention.

Turning idea into action

"Show day," March 26, 2024, dawned with an unnerving clarity. The sun was a dazzling spotlight against the cold March air, a stark contrast to the electric thrum of anticipation just a few blocks away. As the City Permits office and the Mayor's team confirmed the go-ahead for a 7:15 p.m. showtime, a ripple of relief went through the crew. The battle for prime visibility in the heart of America's busiest intersection was won.

Logistics morphed into adrenaline-fueled chaos in the best possible way. We coordinated with production companies, set up global live streaming on multiple platforms, and wrangled excited fans with the help of the New York Police Department, who were just as fascinated as the fans and onlookers by the sheer scale of it all. Nevertheless, they have an eye on everything. As "The New York Times" later reported, the police department not only manages foot and vehicular traffic in the area, they also keep a keen eye on any potential threats, another reason their buy-in and support is so critical.

The hours dripped away, an agonizing countdown against the backdrop of Times Square's relentless energy. The billboards and screens surrounding the TSX stage glowed even brighter as dusk draped its inky cloak over the city. This was the moment they were built for.

Hips don't lie –and neither do timed permits

As the clock ticked closer to the showtime, a sudden flurry of alerts made my phone buzz incessantly. Calls from the police department and city officials were flooding in—all with the same urgent message: The countdown clock was off. It was displaying 30 minutes to go, yet it was already 7 p.m., and the permit explicitly stated a 7:15 p.m. start. We knew there was no room for error; these times were set in stone.

Frantically, I dialed Shakira's manager, trying to grasp what was going amiss. She quickly explained that Shakira needed an additional 15 minutes to prepare. I felt a surge of panic—this was not an option. The NYPD was already on the verge of shutting us down.

My tone was unmistakable, and urgency sharpened my words as I declared, "We need to get the Mayor on the line now. If he doesn't confirm a delayed start and communicate this to the commissioner at Times Square within minutes, this show is canceled."

A whirlwind of phone calls ensued. I was hastily added to a conference call, with members of Mayor Eric Adams' team scrambling on the other end. I could hear the Mayor's voice in the background, a reassuring sign amidst the chaos. After several intense minutes, filled with rapid-fire conversation and palpable tension, we finally received the green light from the Mayor himself.

Just like that, *another* show was saved in the nick of time. In the world of live events, some things indeed never change—last-minute hurdles were part and parcel of the game, and today had been no exception.

We could finally move on.

The production crew was a symphony of focus, voices crackling through headsets in a rhythmic dance of technology and timing. And then...

Shakira.

She emerged from the shadows, a vision of shimmering gold and unapologetic confidence. The crowd, 40,000 strong, roared a monstrous greeting that seemed to shake the very foundations of Manhattan. With a wink and a hip swivel that had become her signature, she launched into her set, setting Times Square on fire with her massive hit 'Hips Don't Lie."

The TSX Stage was her canvas. Every beat, every note, every swivel of her hips was amplified by cutting-edge technology and the boundless energy of the crowd. Her hits, a sonic timeline of her incredible career, pulsed through Times Square.

Old favorites mingled with tracks from her new album, a defiant declaration of a woman who refused to be silenced. The crowd danced, swayed, and cheered its way through "Te Felicito," "TQG," "Cómo Dónde y Cuándo," "PuntPuntería" and "BZRP Music Sessions #53"

The queen and her kingdom

The screens surrounding the stage exploded with visuals curated by the Squared Division. Abstract shapes danced along with Shakira's movements, lyrics splashed across the screens in fiery fonts, archival footage of past performances wove a tapestry of her legacy. The entire square became her kingdom.

The crowd was in ecstasy, swaying and singing in a joyous, multilingual chorus. Online, the live stream numbers were already shattering records. This was more than a concert; it was a coronation of epic proportions.

Shakira, the queen in exile, had reclaimed her throne. And the TSX Stage was the heart of her empire.

Watching from the wings, a wave of emotion washed over me. Every obstacle, every sleepless night, every seemingly insurmountable challenge dissolved into pure, triumphant satisfaction. The plan scribbled on napkins and whiteboards four years ago was now a blazing reality before my eyes. This was our trifecta of entertainment success.

We had done it.

We had taken the most iconic spot in the world and made it the place for the biggest names in music to connect with their fans in a way that had never been possible before. The TSX Stage was no longer just a stage but an emblem of power, a celebrated gateway to global superstardom.

As "The New York Times" shared later that week, Shakira's performance "lasted barely longer than a subway trip from the Port Authority bus terminal to Grand Central and went off without a hitch. But that was largely because of months of behind-the-scenes planning that included securing permits, meeting multiple times with city officials and the police, and carefully calibrating when, exactly, to announce the secretly planned show."

Where the magic happens

In the quiet aftermath, as the stage crew began dismantling the spectacle and the dazed crowd slowly dispersed, I took a deep breath and looked out through a window in the highrise building at the official after-party, overlooking the square. The billboards still flashed Shakira's image, a lingering reminder of the night's historic event.

Suddenly, someone walked up next to me and asked me how I felt. This was it, the moment where I would try to articulate the whirlwind that had transformed my life and the heart of this city.

"It's not just about the music," I began slowly, the words flowing more smoothly than I'd expected. "It's about the connection. Artists crave that visceral energy from a live audience, and fans yearn to be part of something bigger than themselves. The TSX Stage gives them that. And the world gets to watch it happen in real-time."

"What's next for the TSX Stage?" he asked.

I smiled, a mix of fatigue and exhilaration washing over me. "We keep pushing the envelope," I replied. "We keep making history. Today, it's Shakira; tomorrow, who knows? But one thing is for certain — the TSX Stage will always be where the magic happens."

As we wrapped up, the city's nocturnal symphony resumed its relentless pace. The bright lights of Times Square reflected off the glass surfaces around us, a testament to the vibrant energy that never truly dims in this part of the world. We had not just hosted a concert; we had crafted an experience that resonated across cultures and demographics, bringing people together in a celebration of music and spectacle.

The legacy of the TSX Stage was only beginning. With each artist, each performance, we were weaving a richer tapestry of cultural significance. What started as a bold vision had transformed into a dynamic reality, influencing the fabric of pop culture and setting the stage for future legends to shine. It is a place for fans, icons, music lovers, and cultural moments.

From a brand to a cultural legacy

This was more than just building a brand; it was about crafting a legacy, one show at a time. As the night closed in, the bustling energy of Times Square serving as a constant backdrop, it was clear to me that the TSX Stage was destined to be remembered as a pivotal chapter in the annals of entertainment history.

With Shakira's show, we had captivated an audience and firmly established TSX Entertainment as a formidable player in the global entertainment industry. The challenges were once again many, but the rewards, as evidenced by the ocean of smiling faces and the chorus of cheers that filled the air, were infinitely greater.

As the final note of the evening resonated in the cool night air and the crowds began to disperse while still singing, still dancing, still glowing, there was a profound sense of accomplishment among our entire team. We had done what many thought impossible — transformed Times Square into a cultural phenomenon, a nexus of musical innovation and experiential wonder that connected artists and fans in unprecedented ways.

And so, as the last echoes of Shakira's vibrant performance faded into the night, the stage was set for the next chapter. The TSX Stage was ready to welcome the next generation of musical talent, continuing to redefine the entertainment landscape and ensuring that the heart of New York City would always beat with the pulse of the world's greatest performances.

In this vibrant cityscape, where dreams are as bright as the neon lights, the TSX Stage stood as a beacon of what was possible when vision, passion, and creativity converged in one explosive, unforgettable moment.

This was the dynasty we were building — not just a stage but a revolution in entertainment.

CHAPTER 12

The TSX Entertainment Odyssey: Pioneering the Future of Entertainment

At the inception of TSX Entertainment, our goal extended beyond merely entering the entertainment industry. We aimed to revolutionize it, creating a new paradigm where entertainment and hospitality are not just adjacent sectors but are interwoven into a seamless, holistic experience.

Our aspiration to be a formidable force in the global entertainment scene has driven us to redefine entertainment for the 21st century.

Bringing it all together

Today, the merging of entertainment sectors—music, fashion, sports, gaming, TV, movies, and hospitality—is not only apparent but increasingly fluid. This blending is more than a trend; it is a reflection of the evolving nature of pop culture. Cross-promotions and collaborations across these industries are now expected, heralding an era of integrated entertainment experiences and unparalleled opportunities for fans.

One striking example was the 2021 collaboration between the online game Fortnite and fashion giant Balenciaga. This partnership broke new ground by merging the virtual and physical realms, offering digital skins and tangible high-fashion items. This collaboration broadened the reach of both brands, tapping into new markets and demonstrating the vast potential of such ventures.

At TSX Entertainment, we position ourselves at the vanguard of this cultural evolution. Our flagship initiative, TSX Broadway, embodies this new world by merging all facets of pop culture into a single, unified experience. Utilizing digital twin technology, TSX Broadway is accessible to both physical visitors and a global online audience, bridging the physical and digital worlds in ways never before seen.

When I joined the project in 2020, brought in by Fortress as the equity holder of TSX Broadway, I saw an opportunity to realize a long-held vision. With my background in entertainment, hospitality, and technology, as well as a passionate commitment to connecting artists with fans, this project represented the culmination of all my professional life experiences.

Since then, we have met and exceeded expectations, transforming entertainment in Times Square and revolutionizing the out-of-home (OOH) advertising business. Our approach has made the ubiquitous outdoor billboard more interactive and globally accessible, transforming it from a static display of major company ads into an engaging and interactive entertainment platform featuring exclusive content and live streaming from across pop culture.

Moreover, the TSX Stage has become one of the world's premier venues for launching new music, supported by our robust digital platform and infrastructure. It's not just about the tens of thousands who can physically come to Times Square; now, a global online audience can also partake in these launches, sharing in the experience as if they were there.

The future is limitless

Looking ahead, we see endless possibilities. We believe the future of entertainment and hospitality lies in leveraging the relationships that major pop culture brands have with their fans. Today's technology enables us to realize this vision. Artists are evolving beyond their original crafts, becoming brands that forge deeper connections with their fans through hotel stays, dining experiences, retail, and much more.

Some challenges are still ahead, mostly connected to the property. TSX Broadway has been impacted by the pandemic, which led to high inflation followed by increased interest rates. The downscaling and low occupancy rate of commercial real estate will have secondary effects on our business and will be an ongoing challenge for at least the next few years.

While only the future can reveal the full extent of our journey, our achievements so far are a testament to what is possible in the entertainment industry. Awarded with Six Clio Awards, breaking records at Times Square, and elevating artists to new heights, we have already made significant impacts through this platform.

The road ahead is filled with promise and opportunity, and I am deeply grateful to everyone who has joined me on this remarkable journey. One thing is certain: There is much, much more to come in one form or another. It has been an incredible ride thus far, and the adventure continues.

CHAPTER 13
The Art of Turning Enthusiasts into Superfans

A big part of my fascination with the music industry has always revolved around the transformative power of fan engagement—a process not just of attracting ears and eyes but of nurturing hearts and minds into the realm of superfandom.

I have seen great musicians struggle to attract fans despite their clear talent. What is the magic potion for creating a band of true fans? It has a lot to do with chemistry, storytelling, and being real.

Brands and artists today often employ a variety of nuanced strategies to transcend the traditional boundaries of consumer interactions in the modern attention economy and to get–and also keep–the attention of their audience.

The landscape of marketing and brand engagement has undergone a seismic shift from when visibility was bought through the blunt instruments of traditional advertising. In today's digital milieu, the currency of connection is no longer mere exposure but the depth of the narrative woven by a brand or artist through a variety of means and mediums.

A new narrative for a new fan base

This fresh narrative goes well beyond just informing or educating–today, it is all about transforming a casual listener or customer into a fervent superfan. However, this alchemical process of conversion holds varying degrees of relevance across different brand categories.

Utility brands that cover the essentials, for instance, might find the pursuit of superfandom less critical. Their battlegrounds are price sensitivity and convenience, where emotional engagement takes a backseat to pragmatic consumer choices. How many people, for instance, are emotional and passionate about dish detergent?

However, storytelling is imperative for lifestyle brands and creators who are striving to carve out a distinctive space in an already cluttered ecosystem. Companies like Trader Joe's, Lamborghini, Zara, and Costco don't even have to advertise– they are part of the consumer ethos and have incredibly dedicated fans and an ability to craft a powerful narrative without the expense of ads.

The challenge for modern artists in the music industry mirrors this paradigm shift. Gone are the days when the machinery of big labels could catapult an artist to stardom through strategic placements and heavy advertising. The contemporary music scene harkens back to grassroots fan club strategies, which can now be married with the sophisticated digital tools of our era.

Success in this environment is a complex tapestry woven from factors within and beyond an artist's or a brand's singular control. Talent, luck, and timing are the traditional triad attributed to success, yet luck and timing can be influenced by the right talent and a hearty dose of persistence.

Personally, I continue to believe in a meritocratic universe where perseverance eventually ushers talent into the limelight. The dichotomy between success and failure is often demarcated by the resilience to persist in the face of adversity.

Billie Eilish: Defying expectations, finding stardom

Billie Eilish's arrival on the music scene was nothing short of disruptive.

Her whispery vocals, haunting melodies, and introspective lyrics were a stark departure from the pop music mainstream. She wasn't the bubbly, highly produced pop star archetype typically favored by the record labels. Instead, she was dark, quirky, and undeniably authentic.

Eilish's music resonated with those who felt misunderstood and on the fringes of pop culture. Her raw exploration of themes like depression and anxiety connected with a young audience hungry for an artist who refused to sugarcoat the teenage experience. This authenticity, coupled with her undeniable talent for songwriting and her visually striking image, fueled her steady rise from obscurity to global superstardom.

Billie Eilish's story is an example of how technology can help democratize the music industry. Platforms like SoundCloud allowed her to bypass traditional gatekeepers and reach an audience directly. It amplified the power of her distinct sound and fostered a community of loyal fans who became invested in her journey.

She is now one of her generation's most successful and influential artists. She has won countless awards, including multiple Grammys, and has carved out her own distinct niche within the industry. Her rise proves that staying true to your artistic voice and vision, even when it defies expectations, can ultimately lead to immense success.

There is no substitute for authenticity

You can't fake authenticity, and you can't just phone it in.

Audiences and fans can tell if you are authentic with every word you utter, every note you play, and every stroke you paint. Authenticity sparks compelling stories and genuine interactions. It is an unspoken pact with your audience. Chapter 14 explores what authenticity truly looks like–as well as its not-so-genuine counterpart.

For brands today, the real challenge is to craft narratives that resonate on a personal level, narratives that echo the aspirations, struggles, and triumphs of their audience. Creators, on the other hand, imbue their art with the essence of their narrative, offering a direct conduit to their values and vision.

In conclusion, the journey from fan to superfan is a pilgrimage through the heart of what a brand or creator stands for. It is a testament to the power of storytelling, the authenticity of values, and the relentless pursuit of connection in an increasingly fragmented world. Through storytelling, in particular, artists can explore the tools and tactics that can elevate a narrative from merely compelling to irresistibly magnetic.

Masters of fandom: Cultivating devoted communities

Fans are clearly the lifeblood of any successful artist. They amplify voices, fuel trends, and drive the longevity of creative careers.

But beyond mere consumers, certain artists possess an uncanny ability to foster deeply devoted fan communities—fan bases that shape our culture.

It is impossible to discuss fandom without acknowledging The Beatles. The 1960s phenomenon known as "Beatlemania" was a defining moment in pop culture. Their catchy melodies, charming personalities, and groundbreaking image captured the hearts of a generation. But what ignited this unprecedented fervor?

It was music as a movement. The Beatles' music arrived during a time of social upheaval. Their songs, evolving from simple love tunes to explorations of philosophy and social consciousness, resonated with a young audience seeking change and a voice of their own.

Beyond the music, The Beatles cultivated a distinct image. From matching suits and mop-top haircuts to playful humor, they built an instantly recognizable brand that fueled fan obsession. And despite their fame, The Beatles fostered a sense of intimacy with their audience. They appeared in films, gave relatable interviews, and responded to fan mail, nurturing a sense of personal connection. They were accessible superstars.

While the Beatles are the defining artists of this phenomena, many other individuals and groups since then have impacted and changed music, culture, and the world at large.

Some of the best at cultivating wildly dedicated fan bases are:

The Grateful Dead and the Deadheads: The Grateful Dead built a unique fanbase that transcended traditional concert audiences. Deadheads, as they were known, were more than fans—they were a countercultural movement. The band's improvisational live shows, with no two performances ever the same, fostered a sense of community and belonging.

The secret to their success started with:

- **Experiences over Ownership:** The Dead encouraged fans to record and trade their shows freely, prioritizing the live experience and communal sharing rather than controlling the distribution of their music.

- **Embracing Counterculture:** The Deadhead community offered an alternative lifestyle for their fans, who happily rejected mainstream norms. From their psychedelic clothing to their nomadic, concert-following spirit, the Deadheads created a space for self-expression and shared values.

- **Ritual and Participation:** Grateful Dead shows became almost spiritual experiences, with fans engaging in rituals like dancing and trading merchandise, creating a sense of belonging and shared purpose.

Beyoncé and the Beyhive

Beyoncé is a modern-day master of fan cultivation. Her fiercely loyal "Beyhive" is known for its passionate advocacy and defense of their Queen. Beyoncé achieves this through a combination of factors, including her empowering persona. Beyoncé projects an image of female strength, independence, and unapologetic self-love. She champions messages of self-acceptance and ambition, which deeply resonate with her fan base.

Her visually stunning performances and meticulously crafted album releases are events in and of themselves. The element of surprise, like the unexpected drop of her visual album *Lemonade*, keeps fans engaged and eager for more.

Finally, Beyoncé carefully controls her image and messaging, rarely giving interviews and primarily communicating directly with fans through her art and controlled social media presence. This cultivates an aura of mystique and allows fans to feel they have privileged access while leaving them always wanting more.

BTS and the ARMY

The global phenomenon of K-pop group BTS and their devoted fanbase, known as the ARMY, is a testament to the power of fandom in the internet age. BTS has achieved unprecedented worldwide success, fueled largely by their dedicated global fan base. Their secret sauce?

- **Authentic Connection:** BTS members openly share their struggles, passions, and personalities through social media, vlogs, and variety shows. This vulnerability fosters a deep sense of connection and parasocial relationships with their fans.

- **Positive Messaging:** Their songs often focus on themes of self-acceptance, mental health, and overcoming adversity, deeply resonating with a young audience and creating a sense of common purpose.

- **Organized Activism:** The ARMY is highly organized, mobilizing for social causes, chart domination, and breaking online records. This collective power gives fans agency and strengthens their identification with BTS's success.

Taylor Swift and the Swifties

We have already shared a little bit about Taylor Swift's peerless magic. She is renowned for her savvy relationship with her loyal fans, fondly called "Swifties," and her success stems from a mix of relatable songwriting, meticulous image control, and an unparalleled personal connection with her followers.

Swift uses her evolution as a narrative for her albums, where her songwriting often mirrors her life experiences, from her teenage country roots to pop star reinvention. Fans relate to her journey, feeling they're growing alongside her.

She is also the master of secret sessions and Easter eggs. Swift engages in unique interactions with fans, for instance, inviting them to private listening sessions for new albums (secret sessions) and embedding hidden clues and messages in her music videos and social posts, turning content consumption into a treasure hunt. This makes fans feel like insiders with privileged access.

And you can't forget her show of vulnerability. Swift does not shy away from sharing personal struggles and insecurities, further humanizing her to her audience and solidifying the sense of friendship and support within the fandom.

Lady Gaga and the Little Monsters

Lady Gaga cultivated her fiercely dedicated "Little Monsters" through bold musicality, an extravagant visual aesthetic, and a staunch commitment to inclusivity.

She is a champion of the outcasts. Gaga's music and message relentlessly embrace individuality, celebrate outcasts, and champion the LGBTQ+ community. This creates a safe haven for fans who sometimes feel marginalized, fostering a profound sense of belonging and empowerment.

Gaga is also masterful when it comes to visual spectacles. Her theatrical costumes, elaborate stage shows, and constantly shifting personas leave a lasting impact. Her visual choices are as attention-grabbing as her music, making her an unforgettable and highly shareable presence in pop culture.

Even the name of her fan club has a deeper meaning. "Little Monsters" isn't just a cute moniker. It reinforces the idea that Gaga accepts and sees her fans with their unique imperfections, further strengthening their bond with her.

Justin Bieber and the Beliebers

Justin Bieber's "Beliebers" have remained a powerful force since his teen-pop beginnings. His success largely lies in his ability to evolve with his fanbase, offering fans a sense of shared history along a journey of growth as well as:

- **The Boy Next Door Image:** Bieber's early music and YouTube career established him as an attainable heartthrob, fueling an intensely personal investment from young fans who felt like they had discovered this sweet boy next door.

- **Maturing along with His Fans:** As Bieber transitioned into more mature music and faced controversies, many fans remained loyal. This reflects a mutual journey of growing up; fans feel they have matured alongside him.

- **Leveraging Intimacy:** Bieber frequently uses social media to give fans glimpses into his personal life and thoughts, maintaining a sense of accessibility despite his superstardom.

The Weeknd and the XO Crew

We can't forget about The Weeknd–the enigmatic persona and his devoted "XO" fanbase paint a fascinating picture of artist-fan dynamics built on a legacy of mystery and mood. The Weeknd is great at:

- **Cultivating an Aura:** The Weeknd avoids over-exposure, rarely gives interviews, and maintains an air of mystery around his personal life. This fuels fans' curiosity and makes them feel they are part of an exclusive club.

- **Dark and Moody Aesthetic:** His music videos and stage persona evoke a dark, melancholic, and undeniably cool visual vibe. This attracts fans drawn to a unique aesthetic, contributing to a sense of shared identity within his fan base.

- **Meaning through Ambiguity:** The Weeknd's lyrics are often open to interpretation, allowing fans to project their own experiences onto his music. This personalization further deepens their investment in his work.

Rihanna and the Navy

Rihanna's "Navy" is also known for its intensity and loyalty. Her success in building this fan base stems from:

- **Constant Evolution:** Rihanna boldly reinvents her sound and image with each album, keeping fans hooked and constantly engaged. Rihanna is never, ever boring.

- **Confidence and Empowerment:** Her music and persona exude unapologetic confidence, making her fans feel empowered and inspired in turn.

- **Business Savvy:** Her successful ventures in fashion and beauty resonate with fans who admire her entrepreneurial spirit and desire to see her succeed across industries.

The list goes on.

You definitely can't forget about **Bad Bunny** and his global appeal. Puerto Rican rapper and singer Bad Bunny has exploded in popularity, fueled by his musical experimentation, his proud embrace of his Latino heritage, and his fluid, gender-bending style.

Bad Bunny primarily performs in Spanish, yet his music transcends language boundaries, breaking linguistic barriers. His charismatic delivery, catchy beats, and embrace of reggaeton find a global audience eager to connect with a fresh sound.

His bold fashion choices and willingness to challenge gender norms resonate with fans seeking liberation from traditional expectations. This establishes him as a defiant and authentic figure.

Finally, Bad Bunny proudly represents his Puerto Rican roots, addressing social issues in his music and advocating for his community. This resonates with Latino listeners and those who see him as a voice for the underrepresented.

There are artists recognized for their compassion and connection.

Harry Styles' fan base, for example, is fueled by the artist's ongoing message of positivity, his flamboyant style, and a sense of genuine warmth towards fans. His tagline, "treat people with kindness" further fosters a welcoming fandom focused on inclusivity, acceptance, and respect. With his androgynous style, Styles challenges traditional gender norms in fashion, resonating with fans who value self-expression and individuality. And he is known for fan-first interactions–connecting with fans with kindness and interest at concerts and events care.

Nicki Minaj has the Barbz, one of the most fiercely loyal and vocal fan bases around, which appreciates that Minaj is a true champion of the underdog. Her rags-to-riches story and willingness to call out detractors connect with fans seeking strength and growth. When you add in Minaj's unapologetic confidence, lyrical prowess, and bold self-promotion, she is further crowned in the eyes of her fans. And Minaj frequently interacts with the Barbz on social media, solidifying their sense of involvement in her journey.

Twenty One Pilots' fanbase, known as the "Skeleton Clique," is marked by its dedication and focus on mental health awareness. The band professes vulnerability as a strength. Many of their lyrics explore themes of depression, anxiety, and existential struggles with honesty and artistry. With symbolism and community, Twenty One Pilots uses specific colors, iconography, and shared imagery to create a sense of belonging. They speak openly about mental health and support organizations, fostering a positive and supportive fan environment.

You can even see this play in with more countercultural stars.

- **Eminem** and his Stans, for instance, are a match made in obsessive heaven. The term "stan" refers to overly zealous fans, originating from Eminem's song of the same name. Now, his devoted fan base proudly reflects back the performer's power as a skilled storyteller and provocateur.

  Eminem is raw and unfiltered. His lyrics tackle dark themes, personal struggles, and social critique with brutal honesty. He also espouses the underdog narrative. His rise from troubled beginnings to fame often resonates with fans who feel like outsiders or have overcome adversity. Last but not least, Eminem is respected for his technical artistry, lyrical complexity, and skill as a rapper, attracting fans who value technical wordplay.

- With the heavy metal faithful, **Metallica** has one of the most enduring fan bases in heavy metal music, reflecting the lasting power of musical subcultures. For them, it is about music as rebellion. Their aggressive sound and anti-establishment themes offer a cathartic outlet for fans seeking an alternative to the mainstream. They have long engaged in rituals of fandom. Concerts become shared tribal experiences with mosh pits, headbanging, and a strong sense of community. And you can't say enough about longevity and respect. Metallica's long career and continued quality output earn them respect within the broader metal community.

- Then there's **Kanye Wes**t, now known as Ye, and the cult of personality. Despite the many controversies, Ye maintains a devoted fan base that is seemingly drawn to his disruptive nature and undeniable talent.

They admire his vision and provocation: Ye's bold statements, fashion choices, and artistic risks make him impossible to ignore. Fans admire his willingness to challenge the status quo. In addition, his music pushes the boundaries of hip-hop and pop, continuously evolving and surprising listeners. And while polarizing, his public feuds and statements fuel attention, keeping fans engaged in the perpetual drama.

- Last but not least, there's **Phish** and the spread of the jam band. Phish, known for their improvisational concerts and devoted followers, represent peak jam band culture. Their live experience focus is on creating unique live shows where the same song is rarely repeated the same way, prioritizing musical exploration. They engage fans as facilitators: The band encourages fans to record and trade their shows freely, embracing the grassroots nature of their music distribution. And they have always excelled at the nomadic community experience. Fans follow Phish on tour, creating a vibrant, traveling community based on shared passion.

From interest to obsession and fans to superfandom, the entertainment world continues to draw us in, waiting and wondering what's next, what's in it for me, and what tomorrow will bring.

CHAPTER 14

Engaging Hearts and Minds with Storytelling and Authenticity

Artists and brands are trying to get to the heart of the matter with consumers today–they want to create that visceral and lasting connection that denotes a true fan. This isn't always easy.

For lifestyle brands, which seek not just to sell but to embody a particular way of living, the challenge is real. These brands and individuals must weave a compelling narrative that resonates on a personal level, transforming passive viewers into active participants and loyal fans.

The infusion of pop culture into these narratives offers a powerful medium through which brands can connect with audiences and leverage shared cultural moments to forge deeper, more meaningful connections.

The power of a great story

Lifestyle brands stand out by going beyond just products or services to offer experiences, ideals, aspirations, and a particular vision of life. In this context, the ability to tell a great story is a vital tool for conveying abstract concepts to touch the hearts and minds of consumers.

Through the power and sharing of stories, brands can articulate their unique perspective and invite consumers into a curated world that aligns with their aspirations and values. This emotional engagement is the key to differentiating lifestyle brands in a crowded marketplace, transforming ordinary transactions into meaningful interactions.

Airbnb excels at telling captivating stories that matter. They created a Host Stories series highlighting how the company has made a profound difference for its hosts.

Likewise, The Walt Disney Company, "where dreams come true," reaches out to audiences young and old through stories that entertain and inspire with a dose of wonder and magic. They showcase amazing in-person experiences, their work with the Make-A-Wish Foundation, and the magic of Disney moments–whether at a theme park, through a movie, or that first book that entices an audience for a lifetime.

Pop culture: A catalyst for connection

Pop culture is a universal language today, cutting across demographics to unite diverse audiences around common themes–including music. For lifestyle brands, tapping into pop culture allows them to participate in larger global conversations, aligning their narratives with the trends and moments that captivate the public imagination.

Think of Taylor Swift attending her first Kansas City Chiefs game and the immediate attention this drew to the sport and the team for a new audience–pop culture quickly made the NFL more popular with a younger, more female audience.

When pop culture creates these moments of connection, it not only enhances the brand's relevance but also amplifies its reach, as consumers are more likely to share and engage with content that reflects their current cultural interests.

You may have also seen TikTok's branded hashtag challenges, where brands including McDonald's and Dunkin' launched branded challenges that urged fans to create content, use a specific hashtag, thereby promoting the brand to a new and receptive audience.

Crafting stories that resonate

The art of storytelling for lifestyle brands involves a delicate balance between authenticity and aspiration. Stories must be rooted in the brand's core values and identity, yet flexible enough to incorporate pop culture elements in a natural and relevant way. Consumers have to feel that your company is real and that they can believe what you say.

This requires a deep understanding of the brand's audience and the cultural landscape, allowing brands to craft personal and universal narratives. The goal is to create a narrative tapestry that consumers are aspirationally drawn to and where they can see their own lives reflected.

Attracting new customers and converting them into fans demands stories that not only capture attention but also encourage interaction and loyalty. Lifestyle brands can achieve this by creating immersive, multi-channel narratives that invite consumers to participate in the brand's world.

Fans join in on the fun

As we shared in Chapter 7, when we first launched the TSX app, our aim was to empower fans by offering them control over the TSX Billboard through PixelStar, the app's flagship feature. This unique function allowed users to upload videos and photos to commemorate significant moments of their lives on a truly grand scale.

The response was overwhelming, with hundreds of thousands embracing the platform and eagerly sharing their joyous experiences across various social media channels. This genuine and heartfelt engagement fostered an authentic form of storytelling that significantly amplified TSX's visibility, attracting new audiences in a profoundly genuine and impactful manner.

The TSX app wasn't just an app; it was also a portal. It was a portal to the heart of Times Square, to the pulsing lights and electric energy that defines a cultural moment. And we wanted to open that portal for everyone.

PixelStar was about stories instead of ads or flashy salesmanship. It gave everyone the chance to open up and connect with real, genuine, human stories shared in 15-second bursts of laughter, joy, and even tears.

Imagine the thrill of seeing your face, your laugh, your special someone beamed across the 18,000-square-foot digital canvas of the TSX Billboard. You wouldn't need to be a celebrity, just someone with a moment worth celebrating.

A birthday surprise, a graduation announcement, a marriage proposal – PixelStar created the chance to turn these intimate moments into public declarations, writ large in the heart of New York City.

And celebrate they did.

Hundreds of thousands embraced PixelStar, transforming the TSX Billboard into a kaleidoscope of human experiences. The joy was infectious, spilling over onto social media, where users shared their excitement, awe, and sheer delight at having their moment. Sure, they enjoyed seeing themselves on the big screen, but they also loved these moments of connection, community, and the shared experience of turning something personal into something universal.

This outpouring of authentic emotion became the lifeblood of TSX. It wasn't manufactured hype; it was real people and real stories resonating with real audiences.

People who might never have considered TSX before were drawn in, captivated by the raw, unfiltered narratives playing out on the world's largest social feed. PixelStar became a bridge that deftly connected individuals to a cultural phenomenon and, in turn, enriched that phenomenon with their unique and touching stories.

Creating a sense of true belonging

From social media campaigns that encourage user-generated content to collaborations with pop culture icons, the aim is to create a sense of belonging and community around the brand or artist. By doing so, lifestyle brands can transform casual shoppers into passionate advocates, leveraging their enthusiasm to attract even more followers.

By harnessing the power of pop culture, successful artists and brands can craft narratives that resonate deeply with consumers, turning fleeting attention into lasting engagement and fandom. As the digital landscape continues to evolve, the brands that succeed will understand and excel at the true art of storytelling, using it to create not just customers but a community of fans united by shared values and cultural touchpoints.

In today's hyper-connected world, the relationship between lifestyle brands and their audiences has definitely evolved. Consumers are no longer passive recipients of brand messages but active participants seeking genuine connections. Authentic storytelling has emerged as a crucial element in building these connections and distinguishing brands that resonate deeply with their audience from those that quickly fade into the background.

Modern consumers are savvy, discerning, and value-driven, with a keen eye for authenticity. Digital media has amplified their ability to scrutinize and engage with brands, making transparency more important than ever.

Authentic storytelling is about much more than just relaying facts; it's about weaving narratives that are true to the brand's identity and resonate personally with the audience. Authenticity can elevate a brand from merely being seen to being believed and trusted.

Despite its importance, maintaining authenticity is fraught with challenges. Brands often struggle with the temptation to embellish stories or follow trends that do not align with their core values, leading to consumer skepticism. In recent times, Facebook veered into Meta, and Twitter morphed into X; both of these attempts at trying to be more modern fizzled with consumers who didn't feel the passion behind the switch or feel the need to jump on a new name bandwagon.

Lack of authenticity is never a winner.

The pitfalls and potential repercussions of inauthentic storytelling

Good storytelling can be amazing and even life-changing for a brand, while the opposite can be devastating. Inauthenticity is hard to recover from.

Dove: Dove, known and lauded for its "Real Beauty" campaign, faced backlash with its "Real Beauty Sketches" video. In the campaign, a forensic sketch artist drew portraits of women based on their own descriptions and then based on descriptions given by strangers. The resulting sketches based on strangers' descriptions were generally more flattering and closer to how others saw the individuals, suggesting that women are overly critical of their appearances.

Despite its positive intentions, the campaign faced significant backlash–critics argued that it inadvertently reinforced beauty stereotypes, focused too heavily on physical appearance as a cornerstone of women's self-esteem, and failed to represent a diverse range of beauty standards in a genuine manner. The controversy highlighted the fine line between intending to promote positive messages and ensuring those messages are authentically delivered and inclusive of the brand's broad audience.

Despite Dove's efforts to promote positive social messages, the campaign was ultimately a marketing strategy to sell beauty products. This led to skepticism about how genuine its message was, with critics arguing that Dove was capitalizing on women's insecurities about their appearances — the very issue it claimed to address. Ultimately, "Real Beauty Sketches" were less than a beautiful success story.

Pepsi: In a notable misstep, Pepsi's 2017 ad featuring Kendall Jenner at a protest scene was intended to convey a message of unity and peace, but it ended up trivializing social justice movements and the often dangerous protests against police brutality and racial injustice.

Critics argued that the ad oversimplified complex social and political issues, reducing them to a backdrop for selling a soft drink. The advertisement was accused of appropriating the imagery of protest movements, especially those related to Black Lives Matter, without understanding or respecting their significance and the real struggles of the people involved.

This appropriation for commercial gain was seen as disrespectful and exploitative. Further, the sight of Jenner handing a Pepsi to a police officer as a gesture of peace was seen as particularly tone-deaf, suggesting that systemic issues could be resolved with a soda.

The ad's attempt to portray a unifying message was chiefly criticized for its lack of authenticity. By using a celebrity from a privileged background in a scenario that seemed disconnected from the actual experiences of protestors, the ad failed to resonate with its intended audience. Instead, it came off as a superficial attempt to engage with social issues without taking a genuine stance.

The rapid spread of negative reactions on social media platforms played a crucial role in amplifying the backlash against the ad. Memes, parodies, and critical comments quickly circulated, highlighting the ad's perceived insensitivity and the disconnect between its message and the realities of protest movements. This widespread condemnation forced Pepsi to respond.

The ad was withdrawn, but not before Pepsi and the reality star notched a lot of bad press. This example underscores the importance of ensuring that brand stories resonate with the audience's values and are sensitive to the broader social and cultural context.

The incident served as a cautionary tale for brands about the importance of understanding and respecting social and political contexts when crafting advertising messages, especially when attempting to engage with socially conscious themes.

North Face: In 2019, the well-known outdoor company found a clever way to get some free online advertising–by updating Wikipedia with photos of its clothing and equipment used in destinations and adventures across the globe. Even though the logos may have been small, the effect was a big deal. The strategy initially worked as the North Face logo and spirit of adventure was subtly seen across Wikipedia and across the globe, and the company swiftly rose to the top of Google image results.

North Face started bragging about their sneaky strategy in conferences and even in a widely shared video–telling others how ingenious they were for getting lots of free advertising through this innovative idea. Wikipedia was less than amused, saying North Face had unethically manipulated the volunteer-driven site, which forced North Face to apologize, remove the photos, and immediately abandon the strategy.

Clever, yes. Authentic, not so much.

Strategies for truly authentic storytelling and case studies of lifestyle brands that got it right

How can lifestyle brands craft authentic stories that resonate? Authentically!

The following actionable strategies, from leveraging real customer experiences to highlighting the brand's heritage and core values, can take a story to the next level. Consistency across all channels is critical, as is the power of involving the audience in the storytelling process, transforming them from mere viewers into active participants and co-creators of the brand narrative.

Real-world examples bring the concept of authentic storytelling to life. These interesting case studies share several notable examples of lifestyle brands that have successfully harnessed the power of genuine narratives to build an even more passionate and loyal following.

Patagonia: A long-time pioneer in authentic brand storytelling, Patagonia's dedication to environmental conservation is at the core of its identity. Patagonia's approach to building a dedicated fanbase and growing its brand through storytelling is rooted in its commitment to environmental sustainability and ethical business practices. This multi-faceted strategy incorporates the brand's history, product development, marketing campaigns, and community engagement to create a compelling narrative that resonates with its audience.

Patagonia's founding story, centered around its founder Yvon Chouinard's passion for the outdoors and commitment to environmental conservation, sets the stage for its brand ethos. The narrative of an outdoor enthusiast turning his passion into a business that prioritizes the planet over profit has been central to attracting customers who share similar values.

Its popular "Worn Wear" campaign is a prime example of authentic storytelling that aligns with the company's well-known brand values. By encouraging customers to repair and reuse their gear rather than buying more and more new stuff, the campaign reinforces Patagonia's commitment to responsible sustainability.

This genuine approach has solidified its reputation as an environmentally conscious brand and fostered a deep connection with its customer base, who share similar values.

Storytelling is a big part of the campaign's success as Patagonia regularly offers stories about particular well-worn garments and their affiliated adventures–further bolstering the company's sustainable and emotional appeal. They also do a great job of creating multimedia content to engage their audiences.

Likewise, Patagonia has long been open about its manufacturing processes, supply chain, and environmental impact. This transparency helps to build trust and loyalty among customers and fans. By sharing both its successes and areas for improvement, Patagonia fosters a sense of authenticity that appeals to a conscientious consumer base–something that simply can't be faked or purchased.

Through these strategies, Patagonia has effectively used storytelling to build a brand that stands for more than just outdoor apparel. It has created a community of fans and customers who are deeply invested in the brand's mission, contributing to its growth and impact in the world of environmental sustainability.

Airbnb: Airbnb has artfully mastered using authentic storytelling to create a sense of belonging among its users. Its "Belong Anywhere" campaign showcased real stories from hosts and travelers, highlighting the unique experiences that Airbnb offers beyond just a place to sleep. These personal and touching stories of owners and guests humanize the brand and showcase the diverse range of accommodations and experiences available, from cozy apartments to treehouses and castles.

This strategy effectively communicates Airbnb's vision of a world where everyone can feel at home anywhere they go. By focusing on the genuine experiences of its community, Airbnb has built a strong emotional bond with its devoted audience across the globe.

Likewise, Airbnb has a powerful origin story, a classic tale of innovation born out of necessity. The founders started by renting out air mattresses in their apartment to help pay their monthly rent, a simple solution that blossomed into a global phenomenon. This narrative of humble beginnings and entrepreneurial grit resonates with customers and aspiring entrepreneurs, positioning Airbnb as a relatable and inspirational brand.

Airbnb's rise to becoming a leading figure in the hospitality industry is also a testament to the power of storytelling in building a dedicated fanbase and growing a brand. The company has masterfully employed various storytelling techniques to connect with its audience personally, transforming how people perceive travel and accommodation.

In addition, Airbnb leverages its blog, social media channels, and other content platforms to share compelling stories. From guest blogs and host interviews to travel guides and feature articles, Airbnb uses content marketing to provide value, inspiration, and a deeper insight into the travel experiences it offers. This content strategy not only engages existing customers but also attracts new ones by showcasing the potent and inspirational possibilities that come with choosing to stay at an Airbnb.

This is a big part of the company's storytelling initiative of Airbnb Experiences. These experiences go beyond just places to stay to share a range of activities led by local experts. They offer a narrative of local culture, cuisine, and traditions, inviting guests to partake in unique adventures often off the beaten path. The stories of these experiences further differentiate Airbnb in the travel market, appealing to travelers seeking more than just accommodation.

Airbnb also fosters a sense of community among its users through initiatives that encourage sharing and interaction.

From the annual Airbnb Open conference to online forums and local meetups, these platforms allow users to share their stories, tips, and advice, further strengthening the bond between the brand and its customers.

Finally, Airbnb has also used storytelling as a tool for crisis management and adaptation. During the COVID-19 pandemic, for example, the company shared stories of supporting hosts and guests, adapting its business model, and prioritizing safety. This transparent communication helped maintain trust and loyalty among its community during challenging times.

Through strategic storytelling, Airbnb has created a fanbase of customers and transformed them into brand ambassadors. By emphasizing personal connections, community, and the joy of travel, Airbnb has cultivated a brand identity that resonates deeply with people around the world, fueling its growth and success.

Ben & Jerry's: After the death of George Floyd in 2020, many companies put out statements or shared their missions concerning racial justice. But few made as strong a statement as the beloved ice cream maker Ben & Jerry's, which insisted that "We Must Dismantle White Supremacy."

The company further called out the history of discrimination and injustice in the United States and demanded new policies to address racial justice. They asked the U.S. Department of Justice to reinvigorate the Civil Rights Division and for Congress to further study discrimination in America.

Even though Ben & Jerry's is now owned by consumer goods conglomerate Unilever, the wavy-gravy maker maintains an independent board of directors as well as its long-held beliefs in climate change, refugee rights, and racial justice, among others. The founders have even been arrested at protests and continue to put their money where their mouth is by launching new justice-focused ice cream flavors.

While some companies were accused of jumping on the bandwagon or simply offering "thoughts and prayers," Ben & Jerry's was willing to risk business by sharing its long-held beliefs–and then backing them up. Meanwhile, Ben & Jerry's is the number-one ice cream maker in the United States and boasted a market cap value of $101.51 billion as of Sept. 14, 2022.

Ben & Jerry's outrage was authentic, and their actions supported their authentic beliefs. This is another example of a company being real and earning customer loyalty in the meantime.

Navigating the digital landscape of today and tomorrow

The digital world offers unparalleled opportunities for lifestyle brands to showcase their authenticity. Naturally, social media and other digital platforms can serve as powerful tools for authentic storytelling, allowing brands to engage directly with an already connected audience, gather real-time feedback, and adapt their narratives to remain relevant and genuine.

The name of the game today involves staying ahead of the trends, paying careful attention to advancements in technology, and connecting on a real level with consumers and fans.

Authenticity has always been important in storytelling, from the early days of stories that were shared from culture to culture and person to person to today, when these stories can be broadcast via many different mediums and outlets.

Brands must remain committed to genuine storytelling that goes beyond chasing a dollar. The future will belong to those who not only tell stories but also live them, those who create truly authentic brand experiences that can stand the test of time.

The shifting landscape and the currency of engagement

The world of brand loyalty has undergone a paradigm shift. Gone are the days of one-way communication, static ads, and passive consumers. Today, the relationship between brands and their fans is an intricate dance of exchange, a symbiotic loop fueled by the powerful currency of engagement.

At the heart of this dance lies a reward system, where both the brand and fan expect to gain something valuable for their participation.

Let's take, for example, the young woman with a coveted Gucci bag. Her purchase fuels the brand's success, but her motivation goes beyond mere ownership. By posting a picture, she craves social recognition, likes, and comments–a form of social currency that validates her identity and taste. It's a story she constructs, starring herself and the coveted brand, seeking validation from her online community.

But how did this intricate dynamic start? Was it always like this? The answer, like any good story, is multifaceted.

While brands previously controlled the narrative, social media democratized storytelling. Suddenly, anyone could be a brand ambassador, crafting their own narratives fueled by personal experiences and emotions.

Platforms like Instagram became virtual catwalks, showcasing not just products but the lifestyles they symbolized. Consumers became "prosumers" who now actively participate in the brand story, blurring the lines between audience and advocate.

The rise of the superfan and the evolution of rewards

This shift gave rise to the superfan, a passionate individual deeply invested in a brand's identity and success.

Think of the die-hard sports fan decked out in team colors no matter what time of year it is or the music devotee lining up for hours and hours to see their favorite artist and buy all of their merch. Superfans crave deeper connections, seeking products, experiences, and personalized interactions. They are vocal and influential and wield immense power through positive reviews, word-of-mouth recommendations, and even creating brand-centric content.

As the expectations changed, so did the nature of rewards. Likes and comments became the digital applause, but fans yearned for more. Brands responded with exclusive content, early access to products, and personalized interactions. Some offered limited-edition items or even co-creation opportunities, allowing fans to become part of the brand story.

The question then arises: Are fans ever truly satisfied? Is the thirst for engagement an insatiable beast?

While the desire for recognition and validation may be inherent, it is crucial to understand that engagement is not ever just about the reward. It is also about feeling heard, valued, and part of something bigger than oneself.

Brands that build authentic connections, foster meaningful experiences, and offer genuine value in return for engagement will find loyal fans who contribute positively to their brand story.

The future of this dance

The future of this dynamic relationship is still unfolding.

With advancements in technology like the metaverse and artificial intelligence, the boundaries between brands and fans might blur even further. Immersive experiences, personalized interactions, and gamified engagement are just a glimpse of what lies ahead.

But at its core, the fundamental need for connection and belonging will always remain. Brands and artists that understand this and nurture authentic relationships built on mutual value will continue to thrive in the ever-evolving dance of engagement and fandom.

CHAPTER 15

Fans, Followers, and Superstars: Technology's Transformative Power

In the world of fandom, a simple double tap was once a silent signal of appreciation. Now, that double tap can unlock a treasure chest of exclusive merch, backstage passes, and once-in-a-lifetime experiences.

The bond between brands and their most devoted fans has undergone a seismic shift thanks to a wave of technological innovation. Today's fans are leaders, active participants, co-creators, and the lifeblood that pumps the heart of any successful brand.

The personalization revolution: no more generic fans

Remember when an email blast with your name in the subject line felt impressive? Today's tech makes that personalization look prehistoric.

Artificial Intelligence (AI) is the backstage wizard, tirelessly analyzing everything from your social media history to the time you spend browsing a website.

What does this magic trick achieve? Content so perfectly tailored that it feels like the brand knows you better than your friends and family do. From that spot-on sneaker recommendation to the surprise birthday discount on your favorite brand's gear, personalization is a powerful seduction and sales tool.

But brands aren't just pushing products with laser-like focus. They are also curating experiences.

Imagine, for instance, that you are a die-hard sneakerhead. Suddenly, there's an invite in your inbox for an exclusive early drop, which is cool, but it's not just about buying the shoes. It's a chance to customize them with the help of the lead designer or get your name engraved in a limited-edition font. This isn't just about owning–it's about bragging rights and feeling truly seen by a brand.

And when you share your custom sneakers on social media, you give right back to the company that took such great care of you.

Nike has absolutely mastered this art of personalized experiences. Their Nike By You platform lets you design almost every aspect of certain shoes, creating unique colorways and patterns and even adding personalized text. This turns customers into collaborators, and deepens the connection with the brand.

On a wider scale, their fitness apps gather personal data while motivating users, suggesting targeted workouts or gear based on individual preferences and progress. They get to know more about you–making it easier for them to reach you when their next big thing is ready–and you benefit from custom content.

Beyond the screen to immersive reality

Today's technology isn't content with just targeting you; it wants to put you in the heart of the action. Augmented Reality or AR brings your favorite brands into your world.

That new pair of sunglasses? See just how they'd actually look on your face. Redecorating your room? Virtually place that trendy neon sign right on your wall before you commit. Sure, it's fun, but it's also a game-changer, reducing returns and cementing that emotional buy-in even before a purchase is made.

Virtual Reality (VR) takes it a step further. Imagine stepping into a VR concert where your favorite band is rocking out, just for you and a selected few superfans. Or maybe a virtual meet and greet with an athlete after their big win, where you can ask your burning question from the comfort of your living room.

Apple Vision Pro: A glimpse into the immersive future of brand experiences

The launch of Apple's Vision Pro was not only the introduction of a sleek new device, but it also provided a window into how brands will connect with their fans tomorrow. The headset's immersive capabilities and how it blurs the boundaries between the real and the virtual all hint at a world ripped straight from a science fiction film. And considering the breakneck pace of technological evolution, it is almost mind-boggling to imagine what even the fifth iteration of Vision Pro might achieve.

This technological shift holds immense potential to transform brand and fan relationships. The Vision Pro experience made me realize that soon, we won't just "view" content. We will inhabit it. Imagine a world where:

- **Concerts become front-row experiences from your living room:** You can feel the energy of a live music performance as if you were in the crowd.

- **Fashion shows become virtual fitting rooms:** You can virtually try on the latest runway looks and get a true understanding of the fit before deciding on a purchase.
- **Sports events unfold around you:** You can get transported courtside or to the 50-yard line, surrounded by the roar of the fans.

This goes beyond better marketing to offering unprecedented levels of interactivity and immersion. Fans can step *inside* the brand world, actively participating in stories crafted by those brands. The potential for fostering deep, emotional connections with consumers through the world of technology is enormous.

Of course, this immersive future raises questions of accessibility and inclusivity – challenges the industry will need to address with care. But the possibilities unlocked by devices like the Vision Pro are staggering. They represent a future where the line between brands and their fans fades, replaced by shared experiences that feel extraordinary and intensely personal.

Going beyond and breaking down barriers

This technology breaks down barriers that once seemed unbreakable and insurmountable. Geography no longer matters. Price points get more flexible. And fans truly feel the true power of their devotion.

Coca-Cola consistently pushes the envelope with immersive campaigns. During the 2018 FIFA World Cup, the beverage giant launched an AR experience that let fans virtually play alongside Swiss soccer star Xherdan Shaqiri. It was playful, engaging, fun, and it solidified Coca-Cola's position as a brand that goes the extra mile for the excitement of its fans.

The age of open dialogue and super fans

Technology has transformed the once-deafening one-way broadcast of traditional advertising into a vibrant conversation.

Social media is ground zero.

A funny tweet in response to a brand's campaign might actually get a reply or, even better, get re-shared to amplify your voice. Complaints that used to languish in unanswered emails now get addressed publicly, sometimes even forcing brands to publicly own up to missteps and change course.

In the digital world, devoted fans are the new kings and queens. Exclusive online communities have become the fan clubs of the future. Here, like-minded enthusiasts geek out, get insider access, and engage directly with the people behind the brands they love.

Technology has upended the traditional fan-brand relationship. With innovation and insight, it has brought personalization, immersive experiences, and real-time dialogue together to foster a stronger sense of community across the globe.

These trends, however, are just the beginning…

A closer look into the future

The lines between the physical and digital are increasingly blurred.

The metaverse, where immersive virtual worlds will open up entirely new forms of connection, is on the rise. Imagine digital collectibles tied to real-world rewards by your favorite brands or attending live events as a fully customizable avatar. Blockchain technology could power fan loyalty programs with benefits like exclusive digital ownership and decision-making power.

The possibilities are exhilarating, and brands that embrace this future of fandom stand to win customer loyalty and the fierce and long-lasting devotion of their favorite customers.

AI is the future fan's engagement maestro

The AI revolution promises to make the current state of brand-fan relations look quaint in comparison.

Here is a unique glimpse into how this intelligent technology will continue to shape the landscape:

- **The Rise of the AI Concierge:** Imagine having a personal AI assistant that knows your brand preferences inside and out. It doesn't just recommend products. It anticipates what you might like before you even know it yourself. This AI concierge could analyze your past purchases, social media activity, and even the music you listen to, building a nuanced picture of your style, interests, needs, and tastes. It might pop up with a heads-up about a collaboration between your favorite streetwear brand and an up-and-coming artist you'd likely love, complete with an exclusive pre-release offer.

- **Sentiment Analysis 2.0: Beyond the Keywords:** AI can already analyze social media comments for positive or negative sentiment, but the future in this realm holds far greater sophistication. Imagine an AI capable of deciphering sarcasm, humor, and the nuanced subtext of online conversations. This allows brands to truly understand if a viral meme about their product is a playful jab or a sign of genuine dissatisfaction. It's real-time market research with unparalleled emotional depth.

- **Hyper-Personalized Community Building:** Online fan communities are already hubs of activity, but AI could make them transformative for fans and brands. Think of AI as a tireless matchmaker – it analyzes interactions, interests, and personalities to suggest connections between fans who are likely to become genuine friends. These vibrant communities become a gold mine of organic ideas for brands and artists, where AI spots trends and common requests long before they hit the mainstream.

- **AI-Powered Co-Creation:** What if fans didn't just provide feedback but were actually guided by AI in designing new products and services? We might see AI tools that let fans play with color palettes, suggest silhouettes, and provide instant feedback based on market preferences and production feasibility. It's a democratization of the design process, where passionate fans become integral co-creators.

- **Fan Service Reimagined:** Forget clunky chatbots and endless phone menus. AI-powered customer service will be indistinguishable from a real human, understanding complex queries and even a dose of frustrated venting. More importantly, it will have the vast knowledge base of the brand at its fingertips, resolving issues at lightning speed and making customers feel genuinely valued and respected.

Fans in the future will have the world at their fingertips. While some may be leery of omnipresent, omniscient technology, others will gleefully indulge in the information and connections it provides.

Only time will tell how industries will excel or struggle in the face of greater technological innovation.

Symphony of the future: How AI could reshape the music landscape

In a world of SoundSense and Echo–currently fictional AI platforms–a young artist that we can call Olivia finds boundless opportunity. Here is her potential story–and that of many other future artists…

Olivia paced the small stage of her favorite open mic night spot, her guitar slung across her back. It was the usual mix of seasoned performers and those with trembling hands attempting their first live song. Olivia fell somewhere in the middle, with enough gigs under her belt to control the stage fright but still hungry for that ever-elusive connection with her audience.

As a young songwriter, she poured her soul into her lyrics, painting with metaphors and weaving intricate melodies. But as the crowd milled in and out, polite applause was often the best she could muster. It wasn't for a lack of trying, but how could she break through the noise and distractions and pierce the hearts of listeners on a deeper level?

The answer seemed to lie just out of reach, a tantalizing thread in the online articles she scrolled through on songwriting forums – AI. It was a recurring buzzword, a mysterious force whispered to be both a revolution and a threat to the music industry. Olivia wasn't interested in a robot songwriting partner; instead, what piqued her interest were stories of AI tools acting almost like a focus group for the individual artist.

AI-powered audience analysis

The following week, Olivia signed up for a beta trial of a fictional future app that might someday be called SoundSense, an AI-powered music analysis platform. She nervously uploaded her latest demo, a raw, heartfelt song tentatively titled "Ghost on the Boulevard." Her songwriting process had always been instinctual. SoundSense promised to do much more than compliment her chord choices; it offered audience perception analysis.

Within a few hours, the platform spat out a detailed report:

- **Emotional Resonance:** SoundSense noted that while "Ghost on the Boulevard" carried an undercurrent of melancholy nostalgia, it lacked a distinct emotional climax that would leave a more lasting impact on the listener.

- **Lyrical Density:** The AI flagged multiple sections where the lyrics felt overly abstract. While this suited the overall theme, it suggested the need for clearer imagery or a more direct line in the chorus to anchor the listener's understanding.

- **Target Audience Prediction:** Based on melodic structures, instrumentation, and lyrical themes, SoundSense predicted Olivia's music would strongly appeal to millennials and young adults with a taste for introspective indie folk.

Olivia was taken aback. This wasn't a replacement for her creative intuition but an incredibly insightful mirror. It neither told her to change her music drastically nor pander to trends. Instead, SoundSense illuminated areas where her self-expression might unintentionally obscure the core message she wanted to convey to her audience.

Might this be the answer she was looking for (and the solution so many of us are also seeking)?

Hyper-personalized engagement

Armed with this new insight, Olivia made subtle tweaks to "Ghost on the Boulevard," adding a few lines in the chorus that painted a more relatable word picture of the song's central heartbreak. Then, the real magic began. Instead of blasting the finished track on every social media channel with generic pleas to "check it out," she leveraged another aspect of AI-powered music marketing.

Olivia opted for a targeted micro-release, working with another fictional platform called Echo. This platform connected musicians with smaller pools of carefully curated listeners based on their highly specific music preferences. Echo's AI algorithm didn't just analyze what people listened to. It aimed to understand *why* by drawing connections between song tempos, lyrical subjects, and even the time of day users streamed certain types of music.

Through Echo, Olivia's song was discreetly placed into the streaming playlists of about 100 listeners selected for their strong affinity towards music similar to hers. This wasn't about achieving viral fame and instant numbers but finding those few who would truly connect. Alongside that, she used AI-powered social media tools to craft small posts tailored to the interests of this specific demographic – not mass-produced ads, but snippets of lyrics and artwork that hinted at the themes of "Ghost on the Boulevard."

The results surprised her.

Within a few weeks, Olivia wasn't looking at millions of plays but had dozens of messages and comments from new listeners. They weren't just praising the song but expressing how certain lines hit them personally and how the music mirrored their own quiet turmoil. One listener even offered the use of a small cabin by a lake for a future music video shoot, inspired by the vivid imagery within the song.

For Olivia, this was a revelation. AI wasn't her artistic nemesis but a bridge builder. These platforms hadn't dictated or dismissed her creative choices. Instead, they helped her translate the raw emotion of her music into a language her ideal audience could easily understand. This, in turn, opened avenues for genuine personal interaction, sparking collaboration and fostering a small but deeply loyal fanbase.

All of this might sound far-out and futuristic, but I bet we will be encountering more and more Olivias and their music in the next few years.

You might also want to meet Mateo...

The personalized soundtrack where AI creates a harmonious bond

Another fictional creation designed to showcase the power of AI in music, Mateo leaned back from his mixing desk with a weary sigh. Music had always been his lifeblood–not just creating it but curating it. His bedroom was a museum of well-loved vinyl and meticulously organized playlists.

But as the world moved online, buried under a deluge of algorithmic recommendations, that spark had begun to fade.

One afternoon, browsing a DJ forum led him to a discussion about MuseNet, another fictional but very possible platform. Unlike the mainstream music platforms that seemed to lump everything into broad, soulless categories, MuseNet was an experimental AI project. It analyzed your entire musical history–studying your favorites across streaming platforms, uploaded MP3s, humming recorded into your phone, you name it–and built a dynamic sonic profile.

Intrigued, Mateo linked up his accounts. It took hours for MuseNet to churn through years of listening habits, from his guilty-pleasure '80s pop phase to his current deep dive into experimental electronic music. When it finally generated its report, Mateo was stunned. MuseNet didn't just regurgitate his

Fan-Powered Futures | 161

most-played artists or genres. Instead, it generated an intricate web with threads like:

- **Melancholic Undercurrents:** MuseNet noticed a preference for minor key progressions and bittersweet vocal melodies, even within otherwise upbeat genres.

- **Bass line Fixation:** It identified intricate, driving bass lines as a key recurring element drawing his interest.

- **Tempo Shifts:** Mateo subconsciously gravitated towards tracks with unexpected changes in rhythm and tempo.

Even more fascinating was a feature called The Vault. This AI-powered vault pulled up well-known tracks matching his sonic profile and scoured the internet for independent artists, forgotten releases, and remixes with those same sonic qualities. It was a treasure trove tailored specifically to his own musical DNA.

Curated discovery and community

Mateo's approach to music sharing shifted dramatically. Instead of blasting new finds on social media with generic 'listen to this!' captions, he started micro-communities. Each focused on a highly specific vibe or sonic thread MuseNet had identified. He titled one "Bittersweet Beats" and invited like-minded music lovers who shared his passion for intricate melodies with a lingering melancholy.

His knowledge became his currency.

AI didn't replace his expertise; it amplified it. He'd post snippets of a rare jazz fusion gem, asking, "Notice the bass line here? Any recommendations for something similar?" or share a bootleg remix asking, "What do you guys think about the tempo shift at 2:32?" The discussions became vibrant, with users tagging each other, sharing their own discoveries, and building a genuine sense of shared passion.

Mateo wasn't seeking fame; he wanted genuine musical communion. Through MuseNet's personalized filter, he organized online listening parties with live commentary, providing insights into production techniques and sharing the backstories behind rediscovered tracks. Suddenly, listening to music was no longer a passive solitary activity but an active, evolving conversation.

Mateo's evolving musical communities didn't go unnoticed.

Emerging artists began reaching out and submitting their demos for feedback. MuseNet evolved into a powerful A&R tool, flagging potential collaborators and musicians who aligned with the sonic niche he had so expertly cultivated. Soon, Mateo wasn't just a curator but a co-creator, providing mix feedback, suggesting lyrical directions, and even contributing ambient soundscapes to a few promising tracks.

The human side of artificial intelligence

Mateo's story shows how AI, rather than displacing human connection, can become a tool for its amplification.

The bond between artist and fan becomes less transactional and more symbiotic. The fan is no longer just a consumer but a valuable part of the creative ecosystem, their informed appreciation fueling artistic discovery and collaboration. AI helps navigate the vastness of the musical landscape, unearthing the rare gems that resonate on the deepest, most personal level.

The AI composition is a new era of music creation

In the ever-evolving music industry landscape, artificial intelligence stands out as a beacon of innovation, poised to redefine the relationship between artists and fans. The integration of AI into music is not just about creating new sounds or automating processes; rather, it is about fostering a deeper, more personalized connection between creators and their audience, enhancing the creative process, and opening new avenues for engagement and experience.

At the heart of the music industry's transformation is AI's ability to assist in the composition and production process. AI algorithms can analyze vast datasets of music, learning from different genres and styles to generate unique compositions. This capability allows artists to experiment with new sounds and fusion genres, pushing the boundaries of traditional music-making. AI acts as a collaborative partner for artists, offering suggestions and variations that can inspire creativity and introduce novel elements into their work.

Imagine a songwriter struggling with writer's block; AI can provide a range of chord progressions, melodies, and lyrical ideas tailored to the artist's style, sparking inspiration and propelling the creative process forward. This partnership between human creativity and machine intelligence can lead to groundbreaking musical works that resonate deeply with diverse audiences.

Crafting unique and personalized fan experiences

The power of AI extends beyond music creation to the realm of listener experience, where personalization is key. AI can analyze individual listening habits, preferences, and behaviors, enabling artists and record labels to tailor content and recommendations to each fan. This level of personalization deepens the fan-artist connection, making listeners feel uniquely understood and valued.

Furthermore, AI-driven analytics can help artists and their teams identify trends and preferences among their fan base, guiding them in creating content that aligns with their audience's desires. This data-driven approach ensures that new releases, merchandise, and concert themes hit the mark, enhancing fan satisfaction and loyalty.

Live performances are the lifeblood of the music industry, and AI is set to revolutionize this space. Through real-time data analysis and augmented reality, artists can deliver personalized concert experiences. For example, AI can help adjust the setlist on the fly based on crowd energy and engagement or even alter the visual and audio elements of the show to match the audience's mood.

AI can also facilitate interactive experiences during concerts, such as allowing fans to influence the visual effects or setlist through their mobile devices. These innovations enhance the concert experience and strengthen the bond between artists and their fans, making each performance a unique, shared adventure.

AI in fan engagement and community building

The relationship between artists and fans is increasingly digital, and AI can play a pivotal role in enhancing this interaction. Social media platforms powered by AI algorithms can optimize content delivery, ensuring that fans receive updates, music releases, and news about their favorite artists in a timely manner.

Moreover, AI can manage and analyze engagement across these platforms, identifying key influencers and active fans, thus enabling artists to recognize and interact with their most engaged supporters personally. This direct interaction, facilitated by AI, fosters a sense of community and belonging among fans, strengthening their emotional connection to the artist.

The ethical imperative of AI

While the benefits of AI in the music industry are manifold, they also bring forth ethical considerations, particularly concerning authenticity and the potential loss of human touch in art.

As artists increasingly rely on AI, maintaining the balance between machine assistance and human creativity becomes crucial. The authenticity of music lies in its ability to convey emotions and experiences, and artists must ensure that AI serves as a tool to enhance their expression, not replace it.

Transparency will be key for brands and artists as AI grows in power and usage. Brands need to be clear about how their AI algorithms work to build trust with fans, who may be skeptical.

This involves a delicate balance – the magic of personalization should not feel like an invasion of privacy.

To that end, striking this ideal balance will be one of the defining challenges for companies and industries looking to harness the power of artificial intelligence and virtual realities to build unbreakable bonds with their biggest fans in the years and decades to come.

A future harmony: AI and the evolution of music

Looking ahead, AI is set to continue its transformative impact on the music industry. Machine learning models will become more sophisticated, capable of generating music and lyrics that resonate with human emotions and experiences. This evolution will pave the way for new genres and forms of music, expanding the creative horizon for artists.

In conclusion, AI holds the promise of revolutionizing the music industry by enhancing the creative process, personalizing the fan experience, and opening new avenues for engagement. As artists and creators harness the power of AI, they can foster a deeper, more meaningful relationship with their fans, ensuring that the symphony of human emotion and machine intelligence plays on harmoniously in the future of music.

CHAPTER 16
When a Fan-Powered Future Comes to Life

Imagine this: It is 2027, and Taylor Swift is still the queen of the music industry.

She is getting ready to release her next album and tells her fans, "I want to share 25% of the album's total revenue with you!"

The fans go wild. The music industry evolves yet again.

This might sound far-fetched today, but I believe we are very close to this becoming reality (and Taylor Swift would be the perfect person to change the industry with her already well-known generosity and heartfelt connection with fans).

How might this look, and how might it work?

Many of the biggest stars today, including Taylor, Drake, Beyonce, Rihanna, and Garth Brooks, among others, already own their masters–which means that they are the masters of their musical destiny. That also means they get to decide how it goes. They get to choose whether to license the album or release it themselves. They get to choose what to invest in–and how to share any revenue.

Many of these same stars already recognize that the fans are THE reason they are doing so well in the industry and the world–and they genuinely appreciate them. Fans are enjoying special access, special deals, and special treatment for their dedication and loyalty.

It's actually already happening

Influencers are already getting paid to endorse products and services. Kim Kardashian and Ariana Grande reportedly make nearly $1.7 million for a single Instagram post endorsement. Even regular, not-so-famous influencers earn $200,000 just to share their love of a cocktail, a purse, or a pair of shoes with their fans and followers.

Fans today are already getting paid. This new model will simply take it all to the next level.

It is interesting and exciting to imagine how this might look in the music world soon.

Once upon a time, record labels funneled substantial funds into distribution, marketing, and the intricate process of album creation. Recording was costly, requiring weeks or even months in high-end studios staffed around the clock to ensure perfection. The old regime dictated massive investments in radio promotion and extensive tours to drum up visibility, with artists globetrotting for months to promote a single album.

Contrast this with the current landscape, where artists harness the convenience of technology to record in various settings—from home studios to transient spaces like tour buses and hotel rooms. The necessity for large, expensive studios has diminished, reflecting a broader trend of decentralization in the industry.

Radio and traditional TV, once the backbone of music promotion, have both receded, supplanted by the omnipresence of streaming platforms and social media channels. Now a rarity, record stores cater to niche markets, emphasizing vinyl and collectibles.

In this new era, the financial burdens that once loomed large over labels have largely evaporated. The pivot to streaming services and direct-to-consumer marketing strategies has slashed costs and democratized music production and distribution, empowering artists and reshaping the industry landscape in profound ways.

Getting back to Taylor Swift.

Let's say that her new album, My Favorite Touchdown Dance, is slated for release, and she is ready to share the profits with her true fans. She might then ask them to do 20 unique things–such as create a TikTok video of them dancing to their favorite song, update the lyrics to another track, and then share those with all their BFFs. In return, they will receive points that are recorded in a pool. When all is said and done, the true fans will receive a prorated blockchain bonus based on their point total.

The more you think about it, the simpler and more logical it is. The more you think about it, the more you realize that this fantasy could, in fact, become a reality in a fan-powered future.

Today, we stand on the precipice of a transformative era in the realm of pop culture and entertainment. The burgeoning realization that fans are not just passive consumers but active participants in the marketing and storytelling of brands and artists is reshaping the industry landscape.

This shift signifies a departure from traditional media outlets like cable television, printed magazines, and radio, which are on a discernible decline. In their place, a new paradigm emerges and excels, where social media channels and digital platforms have already begun to alter how content is distributed and consumed.

However, the evolution does not stop there. The horizon promises the advent of innovative platforms where fans are not merely an audience but the very currency that propels a brand or artist to stardom.

This future may be a world where the community surrounding a brand or artist becomes their very linchpin of success. The essence of this transformation lies in recognizing the value of fans beyond their role as consumers. They are the heartbeat of pop culture, driving engagement and loyalty that transcend conventional marketing strategies.

In this landscape, the traditional metrics of success are recalibrated, with fan engagement and community support emerging as the ultimate barometer of a brand's or artist's prominence.

The integration of artificial intelligence and blockchain technology will be pivotal in this new era. These technologies offer unparalleled opportunities for personalization, engagement, and transactional efficiency, laying the foundation for a more interconnected and immersive fan experience. AI's ability to analyze and predict fan preferences will enable brands and artists to tailor their offerings, creating a more engaging and personalized interaction.

Meanwhile, blockchain technology promises a revolution in how value is exchanged within these communities. The concept of brands and artists developing their own tokens or coins is not merely speculative but a foreseeable reality. These digital assets, built on the blockchain, will facilitate an even more direct and transparent exchange of value, empowering fans to earn rewards that mirror their engagement and interest.

The potential of these tokens extends beyond traditional rewards. They could be exchanged for exclusive experiences, merchandise, or even converted into fiat currency.

This flexibility enhances the fan experience and fosters a deeper sense of ownership and participation in the brand's or artist's journey. The value of these tokens lies in their ability to encapsulate the essence of engagement, transforming passive consumption into an active and rewarding relationship.

Fan-powered futures are more than a possibility

Predicting the future is always uncertain, but the trajectory towards fan-powered futures is clear. The ascendancy of fans as the primary drivers of success necessitates a paradigm shift in how pop culture brands and artists approach their strategy.

Viewing fans through the lens of traditional marketing metrics will no longer be sufficient. Instead, the focus must shift towards cultivating vibrant, engaged communities where fans are valued not just for their patronage but for their active role in shaping the brand's narrative.

As we look towards the horizon, the possibilities are boundless.

The advent of new platforms powered by cutting-edge technologies will further democratize the entertainment industry, making it more accessible and rewarding for fans.

This transition to a fan-powered ecosystem is not merely a trend but a fundamental shift in the relationship between brands, artists, and their audiences. It heralds a future where engagement, community, and shared experiences are the cornerstones of success.

The future of pop culture and entertainment is unequivocally fan-powered. Brands and artists that recognize and embrace this shift, leveraging the potential of AI and blockchain technology to foster genuine, rewarding relationships with their fans, will not only survive but thrive in this new era.

The power of fans is not just growing: It is evolving, heralding a future where engagement, community, and innovation are the keys to success.

New platform and companies will arrive

The music industry is poised to undergo significant transformation, primarily driven by new companies focusing on deepening the relationship between artists and fans. These emerging businesses are set to tackle some of the core challenges faced by what can be described as the "middle class" of artists—those with monthly listener figures ranging from 500,000 to 5 million. This segment has notably lost traction on major streaming platforms, and I expect, because of the pressure from investors that streaming platforms focus even more on AI and algorithms to prioritize profitability and content cost over user engagement.

In an environment where streaming services are increasingly driven by the top echelon of the music pyramid, mid-tier artists find themselves at a disadvantage. The biggest names in music continue to grow, benefiting from enhanced visibility and algorithmic favoritism, often leaving less room for mid-tier artists to thrive. As a result, these artists must seek alternative avenues to engage with and grow their fan bases, moving beyond traditional platforms that no longer serve their needs effectively.

The new companies stepping into this gap will leverage cutting-edge technology to create platforms that foster a reciprocal relationship between artists and fans. This shift acknowledges that fans are more than just passive listeners; they are active participants whose engagement is crucial to an artist's success. By creating genuine connections and providing value to artists and fans, these platforms will allow artists to more effectively monetize their relationships with fans.

Revenue-sharing models are likely to become more commonplace, with artists offering a slice of their earnings in exchange for promotional support. This doesn't necessarily mean monetary compensation; experiences, exclusive merchandise, and recognition for fans' efforts are all valuable currencies in this new economy. Such incentives are geared towards super fans who are instrumental in driving an artist's brand forward.

Moreover, these new companies will offer tools that starkly contrast with the services provided by current aggregators. Today's aggregators primarily assist with distribution to major streaming platforms for either a fixed fee or a model similar to banks where they collect a small percentage of actual revenue—a game of volume that often fails to genuinely support artists. This model has been less effective in fostering the growth of artists who are just starting or are in the mid-tier range since it does not help them build a meaningful connection with audiences.

There's also an issue with the sheer volume of music being released by aspiring artists, which forces large streaming platforms to filter out releases that do not meet the previous standard criteria of quality. While the democratization of music production has allowed talented artists to bypass traditional gatekeepers and build substantial fanbases, it has also led to a saturation of the market. Many artists may not possess the necessary quality or have unrealistic expectations of their potential success.

I predict that the changes and lessons learned over the past few years will underscore the importance of talent and hard work in building an initial fanbase. Once artists have put in their "10,000 hours" and established a foundation, these new companies will provide the necessary tools to help them take the next step—to expand their fan bases and restore the vitality of the middle class in the music industry.

The potential for growth and transformation in the music industry through these new companies is immense. They promise to reshape how artists connect with their fans and how they can mutually benefit from these interactions. The focus on building sustainable, mutually beneficial relationships between artists and fans will help maintain the vibrancy of the music ecosystem and ensure its resilience against the shifts in digital technology and consumer behavior.

As the landscape evolves, the excitement about these developments is palpable. The coming years will likely see the rise of significant new players who will redefine artist-fan interactions, ensuring the music industry remains dynamic and responsive to the needs of both artists and their audiences.

As we stand at the dawn of this transformative era, one thing is clear: The future belongs to those who understand that at the heart of every great brand or artist lies a vibrant, engaged community of fans. The journey ahead is filled with promise and potential, and it's a future we can all look forward to with great anticipation.

Deep Dive—Sweden's Unstoppable Rise in Music and Tech

In a small but vibrant nation where the cold winds sweep across the landscape, a revolution has been quietly building. It's a tale transcending mere geography—it's about rhythm and code, melodies and megabytes, showing how Sweden has become a surprising giant in music and technology.

The Swedish Music Phenomenon: Beyond ABBA

Long before the digital streams and chart-topping hits, Sweden's journey in music began in the classrooms. Here, children as young as seven were handed instruments—a reflection of a belief deeply embedded in the Swedish ethos: music is for everyone. The *kommunala musikskolor*, or municipal music schools, sprouted in nearly every municipality, offering lessons at a minimal cost. This system did more than teach music; it democratized it, ensuring that a child in a snowy small town could dream just as big as one in bustling Stockholm.

By the 1970s, this fertile ground of musical education gave rise to a phenomenon at the Eurovision Song Contest. ABBA, a then-little-known Swedish band, captured Europe's heart with their catchy tune "Waterloo." Their victory was not just a win; it was a prophecy of the global musical influence Sweden was destined to wield. ABBA's international success blazed a trail for future artists, setting the stage for a legacy defining Swedish music.

The legacy continued with what would be known as the Kulturskolan model, a robust system where young talents could learn, connect, and create together. These schools became incubators for future stars, ensuring that the spark ignited by ABBA continued to burn brightly.

Beyond Stockholm: Small Towns, Big Dreams

While Stockholm might be the pulsing heart of Swedish music, the veins stretch far and wide. Thanks to the widespread network of music schools, talent has a way of blossoming even in the most remote areas, ensuring that the music scene remains vibrant and diverse.

Sweden has produced a remarkable number of internationally successful music artists across various genres. Here are some of the most notable Swedish artists who have achieved global success:

1. **ABBA** - One of the best-selling music groups of all time, known worldwide for hits like "Dancing Queen" and "Mamma Mia."

2. **Roxette** - The pop rock duo enjoyed international success in the late 1980s and 1990s with hits like "It Must Have Been Love" and "Listen to Your Heart."

3. **Ace of Base** - This pop group was a global phenomenon in the 1990s, famous for their debut album "The Sign" which includes hits like "All That She Wants" and "Don't Turn Around."

4. **Avicii** - The late DJ and record producer was one of the leading figures in the electronic dance music (EDM) scene, known for hits like "Levels" and "Wake Me Up."

5. **Robyn** - Known for her dance-oriented pop music, Robyn has been a significant figure in the pop scene since the late 1990s with hits like "Dancing on My Own" and "Call Your Girlfriend."

6. **Swedish House Mafia** - This house music supergroup has been highly successful internationally, known for tracks like "Don't You Worry Child" and "Save the World."

7. **The Cardigans** - Best known for their 1996 hit "Lovefool," which saw international success, particularly in the US and the UK.

8. **Europe** - Famous for their hit "The Final Countdown," Europe became one of the most popular rock bands in the world during the 1980s.

9. **Tove Lo** - Known for her raw, grunge-influenced pop, she achieved widespread fame with her song "Habits (Stay High)" and has remained a significant figure in the pop music scene.

10. **Zara Larsson** - This pop singer gained international prominence with hits like "Lush Life" and "Never Forget You."

These artists reflect Sweden's diverse musical talent and its far-reaching influence in the global music industry, maintaining a strong presence on international charts and at music festivals worldwide.

Sweden's Secret Weapon: The Denniz Pop Legacy

The narrative took a rhythmic turn in the 1990s when Denniz Pop, a Swedish DJ turned producer, transformed Stockholm's Cheiron Studios into a hit factory. Denniz and his team engineered a distinctive sound that dominated the global charts, defining the pop soundtrack of the decade with artists like the Backstreet Boys, Britney Spears, and NSYNC. This it was was a masterclass in melody, hook, and production that would influence generations to come.

Following in Denniz's footsteps was his protégé, Max Martin. Known for his golden touch, Max Martin, born Karl Martin Sandberg on February 26, 1971, in Stockholm, Sweden, is a prolific Swedish songwriter, record producer, and singer.

Martin's impact on the music industry is significant, having written or co-written numerous hit songs that topped the Billboard Hot 100 charts.

Max Martin holds the record as the producer with the most Hot 100 number-one hits on Billboard, surpassing George Martin in January 2024. He also shares the second position with John Lennon for the second-most Hot 100 number-one songs as a writer.

Sweden has some of the most influential songwriters and producers in the music industry. Their work behind the scenes has shaped the sound of modern pop and has been instrumental in numerous international hits.

1. **Max Martin** - One of the most successful songwriters and producers in music history, Max Martin has written

or co-written dozens of hits for artists like Britney Spears, Taylor Swift, Katy Perry, and The Weeknd.

2. **Shellback** - A frequent collaborator with Max Martin, Shellback has co-written and produced songs for artists such as Maroon 5, Taylor Swift, and Pink.

3. **RedOne** - Known for his work with Lady Gaga, including hits like "Poker Face" and "Just Dance," RedOne has crafted hits for a broad array of artists, including Jennifer Lopez and Enrique Iglesias.

4. **Avicii** (Tim Bergling) - Although primarily known as a DJ and electronic music producer, Avicii also wrote numerous hits, blending electronic music with various genres and creating chart-toppers like "Wake Me Up" and "Hey Brother."

5. **Denniz Pop** - As a pioneer of the Swedish music export, Denniz Pop was instrumental in shaping the careers of Backstreet Boys, Britney Spears, and NSYNC before his untimely death in 1998.

6. **Stargate** - This producing and songwriting team of Norwegian and Swedish members has created hits for Rihanna, Katy Perry, and Beyoncé.

7. **Bloodshy & Avant** - This duo has produced songs for artists like Madonna, Britney Spears ("Toxic"), and Kylie Minogue. They are also part of the indie pop band Miike Snow.

8. **Tove Lo** - In addition to her own career as a performer, Tove Lo has written songs for other artists, including Lorde and Ellie Goulding.

9. **Ali Payami -** Known for working on hits such as Taylor Swift's "Style" and The Weeknd's "Can't Feel My Face," Ali Payami has made significant contributions to the sound of contemporary pop.

10. **Ilya Salmanzadeh** - Often working with Max Martin and Shellback, Ilya has produced and written for artists such as Ariana Grande, Taylor Swift, and Jennifer Lopez.

11. **Savan Kotecha** - An influential songwriter and producer, Savan has crafted numerous hits, including works for Ariana Grande, One Direction, and Usher. His knack for catchy hooks and melodies has made him a go-to collaborator in the pop music industry.

These songwriters and producers have profoundly impacted the global music scene, crafting some of the biggest hits over the past few decades and helping to solidify Sweden's reputation as a powerhouse in music production.

The Tech Boom: How Sweden Became a Startup Powerhouse

Parallel to its musical achievements, Sweden was quietly laying the foundations for a tech revolution. It began in the late 20th century when the government decided to invest heavily in broadband, making Sweden one of the first countries to embrace the internet age. This early adoption created a tech-savvy populace primed to lead the digital era.

The 1980s saw another strategic move—the widespread subsidization of home computers. This initiative did not just introduce technology; it embedded it in the daily lives of ordinary Swedes, nurturing a generation of programmers and digital thinkers.

At the core of Sweden's technological ascent was a giant—Ericsson. As a pioneering telecom company, Ericsson not only pushed the boundaries of mobile technology but also cultivated a reservoir of engineering talent that would eventually fuel numerous startups.

Sweden's Pioneering Tech Companies

In addition to its musical prowess, Sweden has made significant strides in technology. Home to a diverse range of pioneering tech companies, Sweden has established itself as a leader in innovation across various industries. Here is a look at some of the prominent Swedish tech companies that have made global waves:

1. **Spotify** - Transforming the music industry, Spotify introduced the world to streaming with its vast library of music and podcasts, accessible anytime, anywhere.

2. **Ericsson**- As a titan in telecommunications, Ericsson has been instrumental in shaping the global infrastructure for mobile communications.

3. **Skype** - Skype broke barriers in communication technology, making international calls and video chats accessible and affordable, paving the way for a more connected world.

4. **SoundCloud** - While originally founded in Stockholm, SoundCloud has grown to become a major platform for music and audio distribution, known for enabling artists to share their work and connect with fans globally.

5. **Klarna** - In the fintech arena, Klarna revolutionized online shopping with its seamless payment solutions, enhancing consumer trust and convenience.

6. **Mojang Studios** - Creators of Minecraft, Mojang Studios has captured the imaginations of millions worldwide, spotlighting Swedish innovation in gaming.

7. **King** - With the global phenomenon of Candy Crush Saga, King has shown how mobile gaming can become a part of daily entertainment for millions.

8. **iZettle** - Before being acquired by PayPal, iZettle made significant inroads in democratizing financial services and providing mobile payment solutions for small businesses.

9. **Truecaller** - Truecaller has carved a niche in communication security, offering essential services like caller identification and spam blocking.

10. **Electrolux** - A longstanding leader in appliances, Electrolux continues to innovate in the household sector, integrating cutting-edge technology into everyday home equipment.

11. **Volvo Cars** - Volvo Cars is at the forefront of the automotive industry's transformation, leading initiatives in electric vehicles and autonomous driving technologies.

These companies are emblematic of Sweden's entrepreneurial spirit and its ability to compete on the global stage. They exemplify how Sweden's commitment to innovation, education, and a supportive business environment has fostered a thriving ecosystem where technology can flourish.

Embracing Failures and Fostering Innovation

Sweden's approach to failure is distinct. Here, failures are seen not as setbacks but as stepping stones. This attitude, supported by strong social safety nets, encourages entrepreneurs to take bold risks without fear of ruin.

Institutions like KTH Royal Institute of Technology and Chalmers University of Technology have become beacons of innovation, bridging academia and industry and turning theoretical knowledge into practical solutions.

Government policies have also played a crucial role. Initiatives like R&D tax incentives and startup-focused funds have created an ecosystem where innovation is encouraged and celebrated.

The Swedish Advantage: A Historical and Cultural Perspective

To truly understand Sweden's dual dominance in music and tech, one must look at the broader cultural and historical tapestry. From the communal spirit of the Vikings to the modern ethos of *lagom* (balance) and *Jantelagen* (humility), these elements have collectively shaped a society that values collaboration, innovation, and a relentless pursuit of excellence.

As the long, dark winters push Swedes indoors, they turn to their passions—be it strumming a guitar or coding on a computer. This convergence of historical bravery, cultural uniqueness, and educational foresight has not only put Sweden on the map but has kept it there, continually punching well above its weight in the global arena of music and technology.

Acknowledgments

To my close friends Fredrik Hult and Tommy Ahlzén, your enduring support and friendship mean everything to me. Thank you for always being there.

Daniel Ek and Martin Lorentzon, your belief in my vision and unwavering support have been invaluable. I'm deeply grateful for your trust.

To the talented individuals at Tunigo who made my dream possible—Doug Ford, Meg Tarquinio, Sophia Olofsson, Fredrik Fencke, Devon Devlin, John Stein, Sean Austin, Christian Olofsson, Jonas Vis, Daniel Galfensjö, Daniel Kullberg, Eric Sernrot, Simon Landeholm, Fredrik Bridell, Edward Patel, Erik Beijnoff, and Michael Freudenthal—your dedication has been the backbone of my success.

A big shout-out to my Spotify brothers, Stefan Blom, Gustav Söderström, and Alex Norström. Your guidance and collaboration have been priceless. I also want to thank the incredible Spotify Music Team for reshaping the music industry alongside me. You're my forever Dream Team!

David Verdooren, for a fantastic journey and a lifelong Friendship.

Phil Meynell, your friendship and positivity have been a constant source of energy.

Staffan Holm, your mentorship has guided me through personal and professional growth.

Ash Pournouri, thank you for your friendship and partnership.

Kristoffer Ahlbom, for your invaluable network and being a great friend.

Anders Gustafson, for a newfound, deep Swedish friendship when our jobs took us over the Atlantic.

Fortress Investment Group for believing in my vision and providing the opportunity to innovate in Times Square. I also want to thank all the investors who have supported the vision from the beginning.

I want to express my heartfelt thanks to the amazing team at TSX Entertainment. Your passion and hard work have turned an almost impossible mission into reality, and I'm honored and grateful to have worked alongside such a talented group.

Lastly, thank you to all the incredible innovators and visionaries who keep doing things we never thought possible. You're the real game-changers who inspire me to push the boundaries because life is too short not to follow your passion. As Steve Jobs wisely said, "We're here to put a dent in the universe. Otherwise, why even be here?"

About the Author

Nick Holmstén's remarkable career epitomizes the fusion of music, technology, and hospitality, marked by a ceaseless drive for innovation. With three decades of diverse experience in the entertainment industry, Holmstén's transformation from a thriving artist, producer, and songwriter into a pioneering leader in the realms of music and technology showcases his dynamic career progression.

His tenure as the Global Head of Music at Spotify is a testament to his significant impact on the digital music sphere. This role followed the strategic acquisition of his company, Tunigo, by Spotify in 2013, highlighting Spotify's commitment to remaining at the forefront of the music discovery. He was instrumental in transforming Spotify into a global music powerhouse, introducing the modern playlist that revolutionized the way artists release music and reinvented how fans discover new music, thereby expanding the global reach of music artists.

Holmstén's entrepreneurial ventures extend beyond Spotify to founding multiple companies within the realms of hospitality, entertainment, and technology. Each venture reflects his zeal for innovation and his dedication to integrating different sectors to enhance consumer interaction and experiences.

He also established TSX Entertainment, a groundbreaking entertainment company based in Times Square. Under his guidance, TSX Entertainment has transformed the entertainment landscape, with the TSX Stage and the TSX Billboard becoming significant cultural icons. The debut performance on the stage by Post Malone earned Six Clio Awards in 2023.

Nick Holmstén's journey is a compelling tale of passion, vision, and innovative spirit shaping the entertainment industry. His groundbreaking work in music, technology, and hospitality inspires a new generation of entrepreneurs, artists, and visionaries, cementing his role as a key figure in the evolution of modern entertainment.